Online PR and Social Media

for Experts, Authors, Consultants, and Speakers

Develop your reputation, get found, and attract a following

5th Edition, Illustrated

Randall Craig

Online PR and Social Media
for Experts, Authors, Consultants, and Speakers
Develop your reputation, get found, and attract a following

Published by Knowledge to Action Press

Knowledge to Action Press
108 Dundas St. West, Suite 201
Toronto ON Canada M5G 1C3
www.KnowledgeToActionPress.com

Craig, Randall M., 1963-

      Online PR & social media for experts, authors, consultants, and speakers: develop your reputation, get found, and attract a following / Randall M. Craig. -- 5th ed, fully illustrated. – Printed version

      1. Public relations. 2. Internet in public relations. 3. Social media. 4. Online social networks. I. Title. II. Title: Online PR and social media for experts.

Table of Contents

Online PR and Social Media
for Experts, Authors, Consultants, and Speakers

Introduction

The purpose of this guidebook is to help you effectively use the various social network sites to showcase your expertise and develop your online reputation. Depending on your perspective, it is either fortunate or unfortunate that there are so many different ways to use these tools. In fact, you could spend all day, every day, working on your online reputation.

The internet, and social media sites themselves, are all in a state of flux. New sites and functionality are always being developed. In fact, there are over 500 of them, with more going online everyday... and others closing up, for lack of business model. This guide suggests the most efficient way to develop your profile, where to go, and what to do: for example, it's not worthwhile for you to invest large amounts of your time on sites that are new (and unknown) - your audiences aren't on them, so why should you be?

Online PR and Social Media is designed to help you get "set-up" doing the right things. Of course, every person's goals and priorities are different, and thus you may wish to do more, or less, as suits you. Chapter 13 provides examples of both active and passive strategies.

Goals

Some key reasons to invest the effort in social network marketing and online PR:

- To amplify your personal brand – and showcase your expertise
- To supplement and leverage your traditional PR investments
- To improve relationships with key audiences: media, prospects, and clients
- To differentiate yourself from your competition
- To improve Search Engine rankings
- To develop a community around your ideas.

Whatever your particular goals, these six are important enough that you can't properly leave them to chance, and that it makes sense to consider them strategically. At the same time, there is an overwhelming reason to be online quite separately from these "positive" ones: you need to protect your reputation against many of the risks (identity theft, brand hijacking, etc). This can't be done if you are just sitting on the sidelines.

Why I wrote this guidebook

As an author, management consultant, and speaker, I have had a fair degree of success with traditional PR, but was struggling to find a way to leverage my online reputation. While there are a number of great books on social networking, there was nothing aimed specifically at experts that provided a step-by-step approach to develop an online reputation using Social Networking techniques.

As an internet pioneer and management consultant (I was behind the web sites for several major market newspapers, international financial institutions, consulting firms, etc, since 1994), I have continued to monitor and advise on the intersection of marketing and technology for some of the largest organizations in the world. And since 2002, I have spent many hours each week following the developments within each of the social networks, experimenting with what worked and what didn't, and have refined an approach that is both effective and efficient for experts.

More of my clients were asking for written guidelines to supplement my consulting advisory work in the area – so the *Online PR and Social Media* series of books was born. I am also the author of a number of other books, including a best-seller, and am the co-author of *Social Media for Business - 101 ways to grow your business without wasting your time* (Maximum Press, 2010).

Some fine print

Change: Each of the web sites and companies referenced within this document are extremely dynamic. It is very likely that some of the detailed instructions and screen shots have changed from what you may find on the web. In fact, it is likely that the number of options and opportunities will have increased, sometimes dramatically. For this reason, focus on understanding the underlying concepts and applying them the best you can.

Copyright notice: The full copyright notice is shown at the front of the book. I'm sure that you wouldn't appreciate others copying your work and passing it around; if you think the book is worthwhile for a colleague or friend, kindly ask them to purchase a copy of their own.

Privacy Issues

PR, whether traditional or online, is designed to expose you to your audience. With Online PR, however, there is a very grey line between your public life, and your private life. If someone searches for you on Google, and they discover that you are an expert in sales, then this is great. But if they discover that you sit on the Parent-Teacher Council of your youngest child's school, maybe your child's school (or your child's name) isn't something that you wish to share. And if you are not interested in sharing your religion, sexual orientation, political views, national origin, or other personal information with your audiences, the double-edged sword of an online reputation becomes even sharper.

Pretty much anything that has ever been on the internet, is currently available – even if the web site or discussion group has long been shut down.

To see for yourself, you might look at the Internet Archives web site, and their *Wayback Machine* (http://www.archive.org). Type in a target web site's address, and it will give you links to the site, organized by month and year, from that web site's conception. (Of course, the other great record of all things online – present and past – is Google.)

Each black bar on the timeline is the complete site, as of that particular date. Go to the Wayback Machine, and try your own site – you'd be surprised what shows up. And you thought that deleting pages on a web site actually got rid of that data!

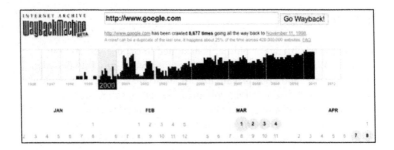

Here are some suggestions for guarding your privacy – or at least minimizing public intrusions into your personal life:

- **Decide on where the grey line is:** Privacy may or may not be an issue for you. A politician may guard their family's privacy jealously, whereas a fitness expert might want to show their family living a fit life. The more privacy you require, the greater your diligence will have to be. The less privacy you require, the more your life is exposed online – forever. If your decisions have an impact on others – such as your family – you probably should bring them into your decision-making process as well.

- **Use separate email addresses:** Use three independent email addresses - a public one, a professional one, and a personal one. Use your personal email address only with close friends and family. Use your professional address with clients, prospects, and those who you deal with because of your work. And use the Public one on web sites, press releases, and wherever you need to use it online. An example of a personal email address is *Jennifer.smith@gmail.com*. A professional email address might be *js@jennifersmith.org*, while a public one might be *Jennifer@jennifersmith.org*. Your public email address will eventually become disposable: once you begin to get too much spam – despite the spam filters - you should change it to something else. While it may seem overkill to have three separate email addresses, doing so helps you filter your mail appropriately. It also means easier updates, if an address needs to be changed.

- **Guard your privacy at the source:** Understand how all of the real-life groups that you belong to are going to use your information. Will they post your name on their web site? Will they post your email in a newsletter? Will pictures of you "out of brand" appear anywhere? Once you know, then govern yourself accordingly.

- **Use the Privacy controls within each web site that offers them:** Some sites, like Facebook, Google+, (and to a lesser extent, LinkedIn) offer robust ways to prevent categories of people from seeing specified types of information. Find out how to use these controls, or don't post anything that might be inappropriate. As a double check, ask to sit down with a friend to browse through your pages from their computer: are you happy with how all of your pages (eg LinkedIn, YouTube, Facebook, Twitter, Google+, etc) look, and with the information that is exposed?

Chapter One: Anchors and Outposts

One of the biggest challenges is the sheer number of Social Media sites that exist – over 500. We know that many of the people who you want to reach – and who might be searching for someone with your expertise, or who might be searching for you – exist on these 500+ sites. If you cannot be found on these sites, then these people will not ever know about you. They will assume that you do not exist, or that you do not have expertise in the area they are seeking. The converse is also true: without a presence on these sites, the possibility of you connecting with members on them is zero.

Yet, there is not enough time in the day for you to spend on all of these sites. But if you don't, then you won't be found. A classic chicken-or-egg dilemma that thankfully can be solved using the *Anchors and Outposts* model. The Anchors and Outposts model works by prioritizing sites into three categories: the main site that you wish to drive people towards, Anchors where you have a robust profile and will spend time interacting, and Outposts where you will have a "thin" profile, just in case someone searches for you or your expertise there. Outposts will have links to your Anchors and Main site; Anchors will link to your main site as well. The graphic below illustrates this, with some of the Anchors and Outposts that I personally use. (In this particular case, I am only showing a small number of the total number of Outposts that exist.)

How to...

Choose one or two Anchors to start, and register yourself. If you are unsure of which to choose, it is likely that LinkedIn is where you should start. Then fill in the profiles, and begin interacting. Detailed instructions can be found later in the book on how to do this. Examples of Anchors are the "big five" of LinkedIn, Facebook, YouTube, Twitter, and Google+. Depending on your industry and geography, there may be others. (Qzone and RenRen, for example, are important in China.).

Outposts are the more obscure sites where you develop a thinner identity. A list of potential Outposts can be found on this page of Wikipedia, as well as at www.Knowem.com. Literally register yourself, upload a picture and profile text, and (important) set links to point to the Anchor(s) and to your main site.

Beyond the traditional Social Media sites, there are a number of other sites that can also effectively be your Outposts:

- **Membership in professional or trade associations**: often there is an online directory that contains a spot for a web address. Use this to link to your main site (or your most important anchor site).

- **Forums and Discussion groups**: often there is a page that contains your "profile". Link from this as well.

- **Paid listings**: Services such as *ExpertClick* and *Sources* provide a range of PR infrastructure – one of which is a profile page with a spot for your URL(s). More on these services in chapter ten.

- **Article credentials**: If you have any articles posted online, or if you write for a magazine/newsletter/third party blog, make sure that your credentials at the end of the article includes a link back to your Anchors and main site.

The benefits of the Anchor and Outpost model are clear:

1) You are more likely to be found when a user decides to search for you (or your expertise) within any particular Social Media site.

2) Vastly improved productivity: your personal Social Media time only will be spent on your a small number of Anchors – not on hundreds of Outposts.

There is a third, even more important benefit of using this model, and it has to do with the connection between Social Media and SEO – search engine optimization.

Google's ranking algorithm is a deep and dark secret: yet some facets of it are relatively well known. Here is how Google works:

- Every time a new page is added to the web, Google indexes every word on that page, along with a number of other attributes of the page itself: the positions of each word, whether the page was recently updated, what pages link TO this page, etc, etc.

- When a user searches for a word (or words), Google then matches these results with its index, and returns results… 3 million of them. It ranks the pages by a number of attributes: generally, the better the match, the higher the rank of your page. This speaks to the importance of thinking through the keywords embedded within your profile.

- What is generally not known is that Google determines the rank of your page by its apparent authority. Google assumes that the greater the number of highly-ranked pages link INTO your site, the more authoritative your page is, and therefore it should rank higher. An inbound link from your neighbor's kid's website doesn't help nearly as much as 20 inbound links from the Huffington Post or CNN.

The beauty of the Anchors and Outposts model is this: it is a ready-built-for-you network of inbound links from highly authoritative web sites. Just by implementing the model, the search engine ranking for your main site should rise significantly.

It is like having your cake (you can be found through organic search on Outposts), eating it too (Productivity), and not having to go on a diet because you ate so much cake (improved Google ranking.)

Advanced concept: While the model divides sites into two categories (Anchors and Outposts), sophisticated Social Media marketers should think of each site sitting on a continuum between set-and-forget (Outposts), and active engagement (Anchors). If you choose to position

Social Media sites this way, make sure that you set rules for how you interact with each site. If you don't, you will run the risk of treating most of the sites as Anchors, thereby giving up any productivity gains. Even more importantly, any community that you try to build will be distributed across many sites – making it impossible for these users to connect, and more difficult for you to reach the critical mass needed for a self-sustaining community.

The remainder of this book is focused on several key areas:

- Registering and optimizing potential Anchor sites

- Identifying and registering on Outposts

- Integrating your Social Media sites

- Connecting online and traditional PR

- Connecting mailing lists or CRM with Social Media.

- Protecting your reputation and mitigating risk

- Advertising

- Monitoring, measurement, and ongoing maintenance

Before you begin, you will need to set goals for what you are hoping to achieve by an investment in Social Media. My book *Social Media for Business* addresses this issue in great detail (Amazon.com, Amazon.ca, and Indigo.ca), so this book will make a very basic, generic assumption: you are looking to grow your profile, as well as develop a community around your ideas.

Chapter Two: Assemble your intellectual property

Blog

As an expert, you likely are producing your ideas on a regular basis, either in a blog, newsletter, articles, video clips, or in many other ways. If you don't already have a blog, you really need one. Ask your webmaster to set you up, or you can do it yourself (at no cost) by using one of the following three services: http://www.Typepad.com, http://www.wordpress.com, or http://www.blogger.com. It is expected that (as an expert or public figure) you have an opinion in your area of expertise.

Tech note: We highly recommend the Wordpress program for blogging. One of the key benefits of Wordpress is that there are thousands of plug-ins, most of which are free, that deliver incredible functionality. It comes in two flavors: one that is hosted by Wordpress themselves (http://www.Wordpress.com), and the other that is available (for free) on just about every web host. If it isn't pre-installed, then your webmaster can download it at no cost from http://www.Wordpress.org. If you choose you're the hosted-by-Wordpress version, then your blog will have a URL similar to http://yourname.wordpress.com. If you do it using your own webhost, then the URL will include your own domain. (My site, www.RandallCraig.com, does this.)

Wordpress is actually more than just blog software: it can actually do all of the content management for your entire website. (In fact, 1 out of every 5 new websites is built on the platform.) If you have any inkling of upgrading your current site, we strongly recommend building a combo blog/website; your search engine ranking will be vastly improved because of it, plus you can maintain it yourself.

Blogs should arguably be the cornerstone of your social media strategy. As opposed to relying solely on the media to circulate your information, blogs allow an unfettered diffusion of your message. More importantly, through the commenting features of blogs, they allow your audiences, clients, colleagues and, yes – even detractors - to leave their feedback. By having regular content produced, you offer a rallying point.

Another reason why blogs are so important: the underlying technology (called RSS, for "Really Simple Syndication"), allows other people to subscribe to your content for their sites. As well, your own social networking web sites can subscribe to your content, allowing you to write once and have your content repurposed automatically in many places on the internet.

It is important that if you do start a blog, then you commit to writing on a scheduled, continuous basis – at least once weekly. If you don't, then your blog will begin to look stale – and so will all of your social networking sites where your blog also appears. Even more critical: a stale blog shows your prospective clients (and journalists) that you are not indeed an expert in your area of expertise. Recommendation: if you cannot commit to a schedule, it might not be wise to begin.

Once you have decided to write one, you will need to determine the goals of your blog. Is it to engage your audiences, prospects, or clients? Blogs can also be used to lower your communications costs by replacing traditionally mailed newsletters and communications. If this is the objective, you will need to ask whether a blog format will accomplish this goal uniquely and how this will be measured in the end.

An important concept is that of a *Blook*, or *BLog-that-is-designed-to-become-a-bOOK*. The idea is that each post that you make on your blog becomes a page or two within your (eventual) book. Here are some key reasons why this is so appealing:

- It is possible to grow your audience by having book content build buzz via the blog.

- Blog readers will likely be a target group of purchasers

- Comments and feedback on your individual posts will help you refine and strengthen your points.

- Repurposing content is a highly efficient way to reach audiences who prefer to consume content in different modes. And repurposing free content into a paid format is another form of monetization.

Action plan: If you have yet to begin blogging, or you have started but are unhappy with your effectiveness (or efficiency), check out my "Six steps to strategic blogging" mini-course, at http://budurl.com/strategicblogging (no cost.)

One bit of information that you will need to do most of the integration is the URL (web address) for your blog's *feed*. This is the address that others will go to in order to pull your content into their system, and is different than the blog's web site address. Usually there is a link on the home page of your blog that says "Subscribe", or has the symbol. If you mouse over the link, or click on the link, you can usually get your blog's feed URL. In the case below, it is http://www.randallcraig.com/rss.

Microblog

There are a number of web sites - Facebook, LinkedIn, Twitter, Google+, etc - that allow you to write your "Status". (Because the Status is so short – 140 characters – the action of filling it out is called Microblogging.) This Status is then broadcast to all of your contact's pages for them to read.

Here is where it can be found on Facebook:

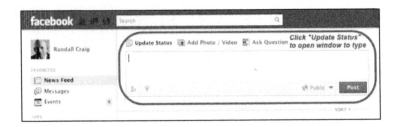

Here is where it can be found on LinkedIn:

On Twitter it can be found in two different places, depending on the page you are on:

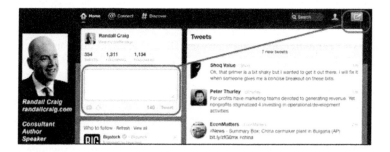

On Google+, make sure that you don't put your status entry into the Search box at the top of the page.

While on first blush these status updates might seem silly; after all, why would anyone be interested in the minutiae of what you are currently working on? If used strategically, however, they can be highly valuable. For example, you might choose to let your contacts know that you are working on a specific new presentation, or that you are busy doing certain value-added activities (rehearsing, writing, attending a course, etc) or travelling. In Chapter five, we'll introduce a tool that will help you update all of your Microblogs all at once.

Over time, your microblogging activities will influence your personal brand; in the short term, it increases your visibility. From a product perspective, it can let people know that you have launched a new product, added a new presentation, or just about anything. Note of caution: Because your microblogging entries end up directly on their LinkedIn page, Facebook page, Google+ page, or Twitter page, overly blatant product pitches are considered intrusive.

Twitter Lingo: The world of Twitter has created a vocabulary of shorthand all of its own, owing partly to its popularity, and partly to the 140 character limit. Here's a short summary of some of the abbreviations:

RT: This is an abbreviation for "Retweet", and means you are repeating someone else's message, giving them attribution.

D or DM randallcraig: Send a private "Direct Message" to the user called RandallCraig

@randallcraig: This is the name of a person. When sending a Tweet with this in it, a public message will then go to the user @RandallCraig, even if you aren't following them. Anytime someone sends a message and "mentions" your name (@randallcraig in this case), it can be shown in your Twitter feed. Hint: within Twitter, go to Mentions to see anything that includes your @name.

Follower: Anyone can follow you, and you can follow anyone. Your Tweets are posted on your follower's public timeline, and theirs is posted on yours.

Lists: A list is a collection of people that you are following, that is publicly available for others to also follow. It's a great way to watch the collective thoughts of specified groups of people. Hint: the number of lists that you are on is a crude indicator of your popularity.

Interactions: This is the Twitter feed that includes anything that has to do with you: Retweets, new Followers, new List membership, etc.

Hashtags (#): People use these (#education, #uk, etc) to "tag" their posts so that others can search for those keywords.

Microblogging tools: If you or someone in your organization begins to use microblogging frequently, there are several tools that can help organize incoming and outgoing Tweets and other status messages. Check out www.Tweetdeck.com, www.seesmic.com, and www.hootsuite.com. While all of these tools are good (and similar), we recommend Hootsuite, as it provides the greatest flexibility for scheduling, delegation, and handling multiple accounts. (www.SocialOomph.com has similar functionality, but is seems unsophisticated and is less recommended.). Hootsuite is discussed further in the chapter on Monitoring.

Wefollow.com

There are a number of Twitter-oriented sites that (supposedly) can help you increase the number of followers. www.wefollow.com is relatively simple: to join, you choose several categories, and the site constructs a Tweet; simply send the Tweet, and it constructs a dashboard page.

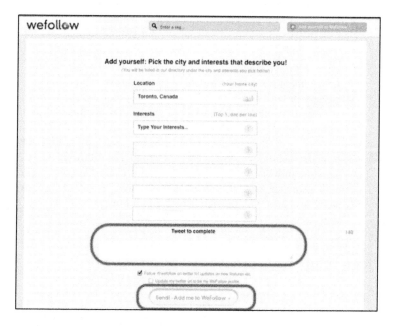

Twellow.com

www.Twellow.com brands itself as the Twitter Yellow Pages - it's basically a self-selected directory of your interests, with categories, subcategories, etc. One of the interesting bits of functionality is you can easily see who is following you, but not the other way around. To join, click on the *Join* button in the top-right corner of the page. You will need to authenticate both Facebook and Twitter.

I've written in detail about Twitter strategies elsewhere (http://budurl.com/7twitterstrategies), so let me summarize an active strategy for people with real-world expertise:

- Only Tweet when you have something of value to say to your target audience. This will help reinforce your real-world reputation with existing contacts, and extend your real-world reputation with new ones.

- What you Tweet can be something of your own (eg a link to a whitepaper, blog post, video, etc), or it can be a link to something relevant from someone else.

- Twitter is actually a two-way, conversational tool meant to engage – not just a broadcast tool meant to shout. This engagement can be with others in your industry, with client groups, or with a specific client. So check your messages from time to time, and don't be afraid to reach out using this tool when appropriate.

- A general strategy is to increase the number of followers – but only the followers who are the right type. Irrelevant Followers will never see value from what you send out. If you do the above activities, generally the number of your followers will increase.

Video snippets

Many speakers, and some authors and consultants, and most corporate leaders and politicians have assembled video snippets over the years: media interviews, presentations, etc. If you have them, now is the time to collect them into one place. Again, like your blog, there are ways to load them once and have them appear in many different places.

If you have slide presentations, these should be assembled as well.

Newsletters

You may use an email service provider (Constant Contact, 1ShoppingCart, Aweber, VerticalResponse, etc) to send your newsletter out to your list. Or, if your list is smaller, you may use your own computer to do the actual sending. However you send it, this additional source of content will be used in your social networking strategy. In reverse, you may decide to use your email newsletter to drive users to the blog; this can be done by mentioning the first paragraph in the newsletter, with a link to the details in the blog post. Some online newsletter services such as http://www.MailChimp.com, allow users to plan RSS-to-email campaigns wherein a newsletter is sent automatically each time the blog is updated or according to the frequency you desire.

Chapter Three: Develop profiles in key social networking and identity sites

There are literally hundreds of sites that have a social networking component. Again, the overall strategy is to build "robust" profiles on several key sites – Anchor sites – and slim profiles on Outpost sites that link back to the Anchor sites. Then, to wire your content (blogs, videos, newsletters, etc) into these sites so that the sites get updated, in most cases automatically.

In this way, your content - which demonstrates your knowledge - gets broadcast even further. As mentioned in the previous chapter, because your web links get broadcast with your content, this strategy has a direct impact on your search engine ranking as well. It doesn't get any better than that: one activity both credentializes you and helps you be found.

You probably know about, and have a rudimentary presence on a number of the sites within this guidebook already. Read the sections on each site anyway, if only to pick up the latest techniques, best practices, and time-saving ideas. Other sites you may not have heard of – and with just a little bit of work, can provide tremendous benefit.

Most of the sites have a social networking component: they provide a way for you to attract friends (or followers, fans, or connections, as the case may be); these friends then provide feedback, ratings, and may even add their own content to your site. Some of the sites are important because of their linkage to high-traffic businesses (Amazon.com as an example), or because of their general popularity (YouTube, Facebook, and LinkedIn as examples). Many of these sites allow you to develop reputation by answering questions (Askville, Yahoo Answers, and LinkedIn Answers), transacting (eBay), or showcasing your expertise (Squidoo). Several of the sites, including Klout, Kred, and Naymz (see chapter eleven), exist specifically to showcase your reputation.

It's important to distinguish between the one-to-many nature of traditional PR, and the many-to-many nature of Online PR and Social Media. In traditional PR, a central source (a newspaper article, a TV broadcast, or even a Facebook Fan Page) broadcasts information out to many individual people. With Online PR and Social Media, we want to encourage, as much as possible, the communication between as many individuals to as many other individuals as possible: we want to develop a community of interest. In other words, we want to ensure that we find as many ways as possible to get your message onto the individual Facebook, LinkedIn, and other Social Media pages of other people and organizations as possible, so that your message gets wrapped in the implicit recommendation from these other people and organizations. And so that a conversation – and engagement with your ideas – can begin.

Going it "on your own" or linking up with existing social networking sites

For those who have a strong following, a key question is whether to develop a community of interest by relying on an existing Social Media site, such as LinkedIn or Facebook, or instead, to create your own unique Social Media site, independently. The advantage of having your own "walled garden" is that it is exclusively controlled by you, it develops a singularly focused community of interest, and it keeps the non-interested out. The major disadvantage is that it requires registration, resulting in a barrier to entry and lower registration. And unless you have a mechanism to drive large numbers of users to your site, you will not ever be able to keep up with the sheer number of users already on the public social networks. Our strong recommendation is to thoroughly explore existing social media sites before deciding to implement a proprietary social network.

Beyond writing your own web application, there are three relatively well-known ways to implement your own Social Network: Ning, SocialGo, and Grou.ps. (There was at one time a product called Google FriendConnect, but this has recently been discontinued.) And there are about a dozen other platform providers, but they are either very small, or are more likely to have solvency issues.

All three platforms offer a unique opportunity for you to create your own branded social network without having the need for extensive knowledge in web programming. They do it at relatively low cost. And they offer significant functionality. But there are also downsides.

The biggest downside is that once the connections are made between people, photos are uploaded, pages are written, etc, it is just about impossible to export this data anywhere. (Much like the song "Hotel California": you can check in, but you can't check out.) Once you are captive on one of these platforms, there are no guarantees that their business model won't change, or that a bankruptcy won't destroy the value (or data) captured in the relationships within the network. Furthermore, any member of your network is also a user of the platform; read the terms of service very carefully to understand who precisely owns the data and relationships.

All three services are relatively similar. Probably the most important thing that you should be thinking about is the reason why you are doing this. As part of the sign-up process, you will be asked to describe clearly the advantage(s) to becoming a member of your network. You will also need to make a decision as to whether you wish to invite the public at large to take part in the network or restrict access to invited guests or members. If you decide to make the network open to the public and want to encourage internet users to find you via the search engines, do not forget as well to enter the likely keywords. To gain an idea of the popularity of different keywords, you can use Google's keyword tool, located at http://budurl.com/keywordtoolgoogle.

There are a number of options to consider in promoting your network now that it is launched. The most obvious is to send out an email to your list, with the web address of the new network. Each of these platforms has tools to help, including the ability to import your address book, badges/widgets that can go on your main site, etc.

Ning

Several years ago, they changed their business model mid-stream, effectively stranding many thousands of not-for-profits who were using the platform at no cost. At the same time, they began reaching out directly to individual Ning members: this caused site administrators to become exceptionally upset, as they had being paying Ning monthly for zero advertising or solicitation. Ning has since stabilized, but for many who know the history, it remains untrustworthy.

SocialGo

www.SocialGo.com contains very similar functionality, and has similar pros and cons as Ning. Setting up the site can be done simply by following the home page instructions – click *Try it for Free*. SocialGo has migration tools available to assist in the process of migrating away from Ning. Interesting side note: Again, reading the terms of service are critical.

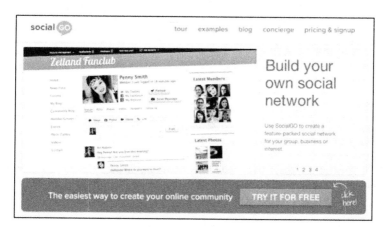

Grou.ps

This particular software platform is relatively new, and comes from developers in Turkey, though it claims approximately 10M members on 215K sites. More at http://www.grou.ps.

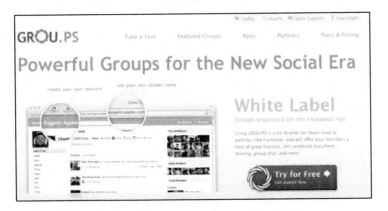

Ning vs SocialGo vs Grou.ps: This is not the question. The real question is whether you have a big enough pull to have your own captive Social Network at all. Consider the following sliding scale:

1) Weak follower base/No ongoing marketing: Do not attempt a Social Network; Use blogs and comments to grow your influence.

2) Emerging influence/Some market presence: Create your own LinkedIn Groups and/or Facebook Pages to take advantage of the significant user base on these platforms.

4) Powerful influence over others, built-in marketing platform, but lower budget: Create a Social Network using any of these tools. Risk changes in the platforms' terms of service.

5) Powerful influence over others, built-in marketing platform, higher budget: Develop a completely customized Social Network to maintain 100% control over content and community.

While the programming and graphic design for your web site is far beyond the scope of this book, a best practices web site would have the following attributes:

- Blog is integral to the site, built-in, rather than existing independently.

- Social Media functions also built in: user profiles, discussion forums, event attendee management, feedback for pages and blog posts, including "rating" of post quality.

- Videos and comments embedded.

- Widgets that bring in content from other social media platforms (eg Twitter, Facebook, etc).

YouTube

YouTube is the largest video sharing site on the internet, and as a result, should be the primary repository of any of your video assets. In YouTube lingo, you need to create a "channel".

YouTube itself is important for so many reasons:

- You can add your Demo video, to let prospective clients see you in action.

- If you serve people whose language isn't English, or who have difficulty reading, YouTube video provides yet another way to connect.

- You can add media clips (assuming you have permission) to credentialize you as a third party expert.

- You can add special video content discussing a specialized issue.

- YouTube content can be automatically presented in many other social networking web sites (Facebook as an example)

- YouTube provides *widgets*, which are snippets of HTML that allow you to embed the video within your own web site. Widgets also allow others to embed your video within *their* web pages.

Of course, the first decision you must make is whether to produce video or not. If you do create a lot of video, then your YouTube Channel can be an Anchor site; if not, then it can be an Outpost. If video is not part of your marketing mix, then you might still consider creating/finding 2-3 clips, just so you can be found when people search for you.

Our view is that any person who is reading this guidebook needs to be developing video content; if not for now, then for the future. Consider these statistics:

- YouTube is the second most used Search engine, just behind Google.

- 48 hours of video are uploaded every minute.

- 13% of YouTube's views occur on mobile

- Cisco estimates that by 2015, fully 90% of the Internet traffic will be video.

If there is any doubt that the future is as much video as textual, these stats should put that doubt to rest.

YouTube Channel Types

At one time, there were several different types of YouTube accounts that you could directly choose: Director, Musician, Comedian, Guru, and Reporter. (There are also several non-public channel types, including Politician and Partner.) Each special account type provided specialized functionality and profile-building capability. Unfortunately, it seems that YouTube is no longer allowing users to self-select their channel type; any references to this are out-of-date. And with the latest YouTube changes, these specialized channel types are no different from the regular channel type.

How to develop your own YouTube Channel:

1) YouTube is owned by Google, which means that if you already have a Google ID (usually a gmail account), you already are half-way there. If you don't, then head over to http://www.YouTube.com and sign up. (Either sign in, or create a new Google account for use with YouTube.)

Start by clicking the link that says *Create Account*, near the top right corner of the YouTube home page. (Remember that YouTube is constantly changing the user interface, so it might not appear on your computer exactly as it is shown.) You will then come to a series of registration pages:

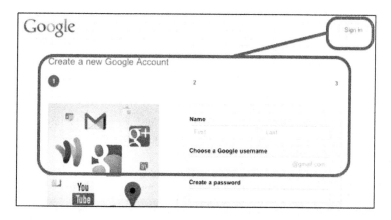

Be careful when you choose your "username", as it can NEVER be changed. It is better to use the name that you are hoping to become your brand, to ensure that your Channel can be found. (If you have many, many videos, consider having a few channels, one under your personal name, the other under the name of your company/book, etc)

If you have an old YouTube account and you sign in with your old YouTube username, they will force you to connect this account to a Google account; if you don't have a Google account, it will require that you sign up for one before proceeding.

2) As part of the sign-up process, you will need to verify that you indeed were the person that set up the account, so Google will send an email to your address for validation.

3) There are three basic steps that you need to go through to be 100% operational. First you will need to customize your account, then customize your channel, then upload videos to your channel. (Of course, the most important step is to market your channel...)

a) Customizing your account:

To show the Channel controls, click on your *Account Name* (1) to expose the options, then click *Settings* (2) in order to begin customizing.

On the next page, click on *Profile Setup* to begin. To upload an image of yourself, your book, your logo, or other appropriate picture, click on the button *Change Picture*.

Of the three options below, you will likely want to upload your own image: click *Browse* to find the graphic from your local computer to upload, and then click *Save Changes* to finish. Note that there can be a delay between when you upload the image and when it appears on your page.

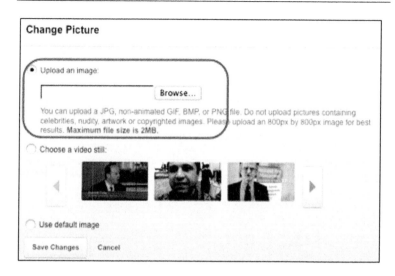

Continue by filling in the blanks, and then click *Save Changes*. Don't forget to put in your Website URL – whether YouTube is an Anchor or Outpost, you still want it to point to your main web site. (Note: if you do not have a main website, consider putting your LinkedIn profile URL here.)

There are many, many options that can be set, which can be accessed through the menu choices in the left navigation. There are a small number of them that are critical. Click on *Sharing* to begin.

YouTube allows you to automatically notify several other Social Media sites (such as Orkut, Twitter and Facebook) with any video changes to your YouTube channel. Click on the *Facebook* link and the *Twitter* link to start the sharing process: windows will open that may ask you to sign in again, and then confirm your intention to connect the services. Note: you will need accounts on both of these services in order to make the connection. Instructions on how to do this are shown later in this book.

On the Facebook authorization screen, click *Allow*.

On the Twitter authorization screen, click on *Authorize app*.

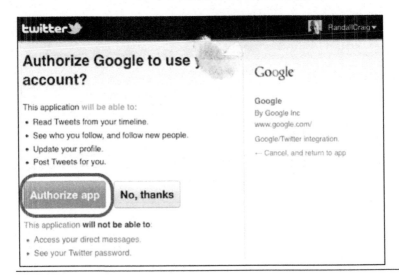

When you are finished, click *Save Changes* at the bottom of the page.

The other options on the left-hand menu are all relatively innocuous, and you can probably leave them as they are until later. The only ones that might be of greater interest are:

Email options: go into this area to control the number of auto-generated emails from YouTube. My recommendation is to turn off the YouTube Newsletters, but turn on Automatic email notifications.

Mobile: In this area is a special email address – if you send a video from your smart phone to this address, it is auto-posted to your Channel. Timesaving suggestion: put this address into your smartphone's address book, under "YouTube".

b) Customizing your channel:

On your channel page, click the button that says Edit Channel, to change basic formatting. Then change the background color to suit. If you wish, you can load a background image that "tiles" behind the page content instead. The other tabs, *Info and Settings* and *Featured Tab*, contain important information that also appears within the channel. In the *Info and Settings* area, make sure that you fill out as much information as possible, including the Title, Description and Tags: this will determine how easily your Channel can be found. We recommend that the *Default Tab* dropdown be set as *Feed Tab*. And make sure that *Visibility* is selected, or else the channel will not be accessible publicly on YouTube. (You may wish to set it as invisible until you are ready to go live with your channel.)

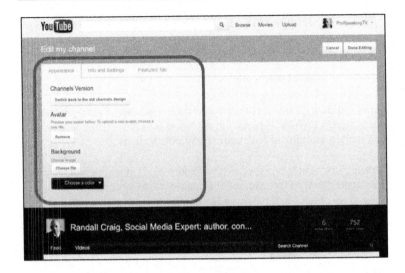

In the *Featured Tab* area, we recommend that this functionality NOT be initially enabled, as it provides even more choice/distraction to your viewers. Once you have a significant number of videos, then the choices under the *Featured Tab* will help you better curate your content.

Once you've filled this information out, click *Done Editing* in the top right corner. You're then ready to edit the channel content. In the right hand corner of the channel content column, click *Edit*.

This exposes the area where you can choose to show (or not) Google+, Twitter and Facebook icons. As well, you can add your description and additional web URLs. This is a critical step in wiring your sites together, and generating cross-traffic between them. (Anchors and Outposts?)

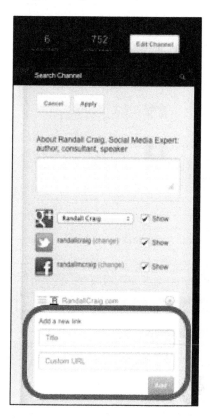

c) Once your Channel is set up, you can then **begin uploading your videos**. Click in the Top right hand corner to begin the *Upload* process.

This will bring you to an intermediate page, where you can click *Select Files from your computer* to actually begin the Upload process. You can also drag files onto your browser, or use several other options.

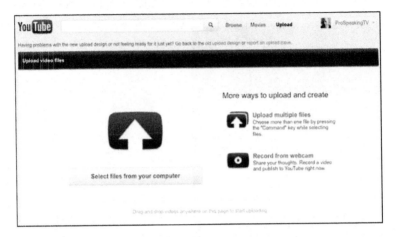

For each video, you will need to provide some background information.

As the video is being uploaded, fill in the blanks for the title, description, tags, and category; all of these will be searched if someone is looking for your expertise. Then click *Save Changes*. Hint: Put your name within the title! Later, when the video is uploaded, you can choose which thumbnail image to use as the keyframe that people see.

One of the advantages (and problems) with YouTube is that there is a risk that people may write nasty comments on your video. I have seen this a number of times with my clients, and it is a constant source of frustration. You will need to edit further details to address this risk.

There is also a question of balancing risk against engagement, and workload. The more "open" you are, the more user engagement there will be with the site (and therefore with you), and the more likely that your content will be passed along to others. On the other hand, the more open you are, the more ongoing time management you will need to commit.

There are currently two ways to change these settings. The easiest way is to click on a video (when you are logged in), then click on Edit Info.

This brings up the Inline editing controls; the entire page is editable. Other buttons (*Video Thumbnail*, for example) allow other settings to be modified. Generally I opt to automatically allow comments, in the hopes of increasing engagement.

Again: the more completely this meta data is filled in, the more findable your video will be.

Bonus Idea: YouTube has the concept of Favorites and Playlists. You can put your videos into both of these categories: it's just another way for users to find your content. Look for the dropdown button just under the video: it says *+Add to*.

LinkedIn

LinkedIn has blossomed from an online resume, to a key mechanism for you to both do outbound marketing, and for others to connect to you. It is also the first Anchor Site that you should build out. Here are the key things that you need to do:

1) Sign up for the service. Go to http://www.LinkedIn.com.

2) Add summary, experience, education, interests, and honors/awards. Under the *Profile* menu, choose *Edit Profile*. Wherever there is an *Edit* button, fill in the blanks. If you are doing this for the first time, there is a wizard that reminds you to fill in all of the appropriate blanks. If you want a bit more directed help, click the *Improve your Profile* button on the right-hand side.

Bonus Tip: If you work in other languages, you can create additional profiles in these languages. To do this, select *Create your profile in another language*, which is in the right-hand column. This is actually quite important, as this allows you to have searchable profile with keywords in the other language.

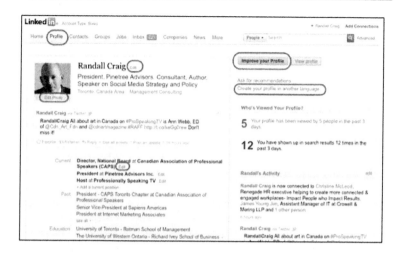

3) Add your web sites. Instead of choosing the generic titles that are offered, such as "My Website", "My Company", etc, choose "Other" from the drop-down list. This will allow you to name the website specifically. In the example below, I have labeled one of the items "Two of my Social Media Books", which is far more descriptive than the alternatives. While you're on this page, fill in the other items with keyword rich content: people will find your profile when their searches include these keywords. Don't forget to click on the *Save Changes* button on the bottom of the page.

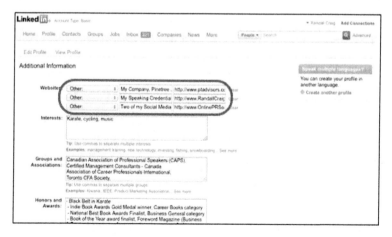

4) Upload your contacts. Under the Contacts menu, select *Add Connections*. You will be brought to a screen that provides four options for adding contacts. On the right-hand side of the page is the mechanism for adding contacts' email addresses manually: ignore this completely.

The most efficient way to add connections is to give LinkedIn access to your email addresses. If you have webmail (eg Gmail, Hotmail, Yahoo! mail, or dozens of others) you can easily type in your email address and password, and LinkedIn will fetch the names/email addresses. Important: it doesn't automatically send anything, but rather, puts these into a holding tank, for you to select who specifically will get an invite.

Alternatively, if you use a PC or Mac-based email program (eg Outlook, Apple Mail, etc), you can use that program to export a file of your contacts, then import this file into LinkedIn. Like the webmail import, LinkedIn will not auto-send an invite without you first selecting who should receive it.

No matter the method of input, make sure that you change the boilerplate email text from the "standard" that LinkedIn suggests. There is nothing wrong with LinkedIn's standard text, except that a bit of customization shows effort, something that most recipients would appreciate.

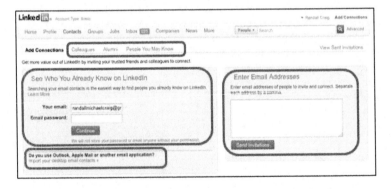

From this screen, you can also click on the tabs to search for colleagues, alumni, and other people you may know. The first two do a search of the LinkedIn database based on the companies that you've added and the schools you've attended. The last tab makes suggestions based on a proprietary LinkedIn algorithm.

Within hours, expect to receive notifications that your contacts have approved your connection request. At this point, you will be connected with each other; you'll be able to see more of their profile, including, in most cases, all of *their* connections.

Note for Microsoft Outlook for Windows users: LinkedIn has a powerful plug-in that shares data from LinkedIn from within Outlook. Go to http://budurl.com/LinkedinOutlook for more details and to download.

5) Review your connection's connections. For each of your connections, click through to their profile. Then click on *Connections*, in the middle of the page, in order to bring up the list of people that they know. (If you click on *Connections* from the top *Contacts* navigation menu, you will see your connections, not theirs!)

If you know anyone on that list (that isn't already a connection), click on +*Connect*, which can be found on the right side of the page next to each name. This will give you a few choices and instructions on how to proceed. The overall goal is to look through your connections' list, and connect through to others that you already know, in order to widen your connection base further.

There is a debate in the LinkedIn community over how to decide about inviting or accepting invitations to/from others. One camp suggests that it is in your best interest to grow your list of connections as large as possible, without regard to how well (or if) you know each connection in the real world. You will often see the term LION (LinkedIn Open Networker) beside their name. The other camp believes that LinkedIn should be used exclusively to connect with those who you already have a relationship with, and that you would feel comfortable making a recommendation or referral. Here's our recommendation: set a specific policy on who to accept or not.

For recruiters, they may wish to have as many as possible, in order to use LinkedIn as their de facto resume database. For senior managers or those with some public profile, the recommendation is to accept or ask for LinkedIn connections only with those who you have a real relationship with. In my own case, I have two rules: I only accept connections from clients and personal relationships, where I am willing to refer business to, or where I will "jump" if they ask a favor. I will also accept relationships with members from the professional associations that I belong too, as I assume that eventually I will have a relationship with them.

If you insist on inviting each and every contact of your contacts, then you will likely strain your relationships... and put your reputation at risk.

6) Request Recommendations. When potential clients or the media check you out, having a history of positive recommendations posted within your profile is a great way to credentialize yourself. There are several entry points to make the request, but it is highly recommend that you do one thing first: pick up the phone, and have a conversation with the person you are hoping to ask. Not only does this strengthen and renew the relationship, but if there are any doubts, it's better to find out then and there. The last thing you want is to think someone might give you a great endorsement, but the reality is the opposite. The phone call also helps you to refresh the person's recollection of how you worked together... which will result in a better endorsement.

Once they've agreed over the phone to endorse you, then the fastest way to translate this into LinkedIn is to click on the *Recommendations* link under the *Profile* menu in the top navigation. Then click on the *Ask to be endorsed* link for the particular position that you are looking to be endorsed for.

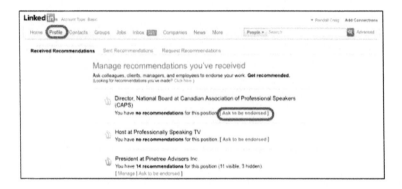

7) Add applications and sections. This is a powerful part of LinkedIn that typically gets ignored; adding applications gives more functionality to your profile, and allows you to pull in your content from other sources. Adding sections gives you the opportunity to add structured information (Honors, Projects, Courses, Volunteer Experience, etc).

Under the *More* menu, select *Get More Applications...* to see the Applications that are available.

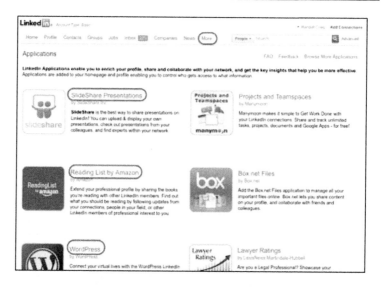

If you have a blog, add either the *WordPress* application or the *Blog Link* application, both of which will pull in your blog posts. Adding one of these apps is arguably the most important thing you can do with your LinkedIn profile, as it allows anyone who is looking at you to not only see your experience, but also see how you think. You will need your RSS Feed URL to set this up.

If you have written a book, add the *Reading List by Amazon* application. This will allow you to add your books directly to your profile (assuming they are available on Amazon.com). If you don't have any books, then you can use this to highlight books that have been influential to you.

If you have slide presentations that you want to share, add *SlideShare Presentations*. You will need to register at http://www.slideshare.net to use this application. Essentially, you will upload your presentations to the SlideShare web site, then access those presentations both on the SlideShare site, and also within LinkedIn when using the SlideShare application.

An alternative to Slideshare is to use the *Google Presentation* application, which does this same thing, but brings in presentations hosted within Google Docs. (To use the Google Presentation app, you will need a free Google account.)

There seems to be a love-hate relationship between Google and LinkedIn that has an interesting spin for those who use video. One of the obscure benefits of using *Google Presentation* was that it allowed you to embed a YouTube video within one of your slides, and then embed that one-slide presentation into LinkedIn. Unfortunately, this functionality has not been working consistently, and currently seems broken. Or perhaps more likely, it is a casualty in the war between the two Social Media giants. In case this becomes available in the future, here is how to get it to work:

1) Upload a video of yourself to your YouTube account. See the previous chapter for details.

2) Go into Google Docs, and create a new presentation. Rename it from "Untitled Presentation" to something more relevant to you. Do this by clicking on the name of the document near the top of the screen. Next, add the video: under the *Insert* menu, choose *Video...*

3) When the YouTube dialog box pops up, search for your name, looking for the video that you previously created. Click *Select Video*. This should insert the video into the middle of your presentation.

4) Stretch the video to fill as much of the slide as possible. Do this by grabbing the corners of the video itself.

To add an application or new section to your LinkedIn Profile (we'll use Google Presentation as an example):

1) Go to *Edit Profile*, under the *Profile* menu.

2) Scroll down the page until you see *Add Sections*. Click it, and the *Add Sections* Dialog box will appear. Scroll through the available sections, until you see Google Presentation. Select this app, then click on *Add Application*. (Note: This Dialog box is also where you can see the list of available sections that can be added; you'll want to spend some time in this area exploring.)

3) At this point, the application has been added to your Profile, but you need to tell the application *which* Google presentation you would like to have appear. Click the *Get Started* button to begin.

4) Select the presentation from the list and click *Post to profile*; if you're not signed into your Google account, you will be prompted to do so first.

After completing these steps, you should double-check your Profile page to ensure that the video actually appears. If there is a message that says "currently there is no presentation posted", then that means that Google and LinkedIn still haven't figured out how to cooperate, and that that you should probably remove the application from your profile.

Note: if having video appear directly on your LinkedIn profile is critical, then a similar process can be used with Slideshare, however video streaming in LinkedIn is only available in the Pro version. Check it out at http://www.slideshare.net/business/premium/plans

8) Add Groups. Groups are a powerful way to connect to the communities that matter to you. When you are a member of a LinkedIn group, you have the opportunity to participate in discussions, ask/answer questions, view group news, etc. As an authority in your area, it would seem strange if you were disconnected from the 'buzz' that is happening all around you. Group membership helps in another way as well: you have the opportunity to be found.

There are two types of groups: Open, and Closed. Closed groups require the group's owner to approve your entry, while with Open groups, anything (and anyone) goes.

The fastest, most efficient way to find relevant groups is through the "Search Groups" at the top right hand corner of the page., or by going to the *Groups Directory* under the *Groups* menu At the time of writing, there were over 1.2 million distinctive LinkedIn groups – so there are a significant number of places you might consider.

There is a limit to the number of groups you can join: currently that limit is 50. We recommend that you only join those groups that are relevant to you, and leave those that aren't. Your inactivity sends a message as well.

Here are some different ways to look at the groups, and how you decide which ones to join:

- **Alumni groups**, to connect with former classmates. Search for your school name or program name.

- **Professional associations' own groups**, for support and "shop talk" about your industry. For example, I am a member of the NSA, GSF, and CAPS groups as a professional speaker, and am a member of the CMC group, as a management consultant.

- **Functional groups or industry groups**, again for support and discussion on relevant issues: there are groups on every functional area (marketing, sales, finance, supply chain, etc), and every industry (banking, insurance, not-for-profits, etc).

- **Client groups**: These are the groups where your prospective clients would spend their time. Your participation in this type of group is not to "sell", which is considered crass, but to demonstrate your expertise through participation in the conversation.

- **Vendor groups:** These are groups, usually set up by a vendor, where people who use a particular software or machinery spend their time for support, and where the vendor can test-drive new ideas.

- **PR-oriented groups:** Make sure that you add groups for HARO and ExpertClick, which will help you with respect to profile-building. Later in this guidebook we will discuss HARO and ExpertClick in greater detail, and the linkage between traditional PR and online PR.

Finally, you might consider creating a group of your own. If your primary audience "lives" on LinkedIn, creating a group here might make sense as an alternative to Ning, SocialGo or Grou.ps. From the *Groups Directory* page (see above), click the button that says *Create a Group.* (Remember first to define the purpose of the group, and allow adequate time to manage it!)

Once you do join a group, there is a question of whether you want the group name and logo visible on your Profile page. My recommendation is to choose wisely, as this has a direct impact on your brand. To change the visibility of groups, under the *Profile* menu, choose *Edit Profile*, then scroll down to the bottom of your Profile, to where your groups are listed. Next to every group name, there is a link to change visibility; click it to make it visible or not.

 CFA Institute Members is not visible on your profile. Change visibility.

 CSAE Trillium Chapter is visible on your profile. Change visibility.

 Canadian Association of Management Consultants (CMC-Canada) is visible on your profile. Change visibility.

CAPS Canadian Association of Professional Speakers - CAPS is visible on your profile. Change visibility.

9) Choose a URL for your public profile. To directly access your public profile, LinkedIn generates a specific-for-you URL. Unfortunately, it is obscure – fortunately it something that you can customize. Here's how: In the top-right corner, under your name is a drop-down menu; select *Settings.* In the screen that comes up, you will want to click *Edit your public profile*, which is in the Profile section of the preferences area.

On the Public Profile page – this is what is indexed by Google and is shown beyond your network – there is a place in the right hand column where you can choose a custom URL for your profile.

Click Customize your public profile URL to make your choice.

LinkedIn Trivia: Every LinkedIn user has a serial number, starting from the first person (1), to the most recent. The lower your number, the longer you've been using the system. Here's how to find your LinkedIn number: Click on the LinkedIn *Home* menu button, then click on *View Profile*, which is under the *Profile* menu. Now, look carefully at the URL; you will see "id=" within it – that's your number! (Mine is 1,566,001; the most recent is currently north of 150 million.)

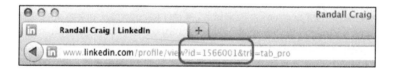

Facebook

Every Facebook user has a personal page. Once this is created, then that user can create a "Fan Page" to represent their official presence, company, or brand. More on Facebook Fan Pages in the next section.

Facebook personal pages are primarily a way for others to connect with you on the personal dimension. It does, however, present several business-related opportunities, depending on your area of expertise and your target audiences. The general strategy you should for Facebook is to allow people who are "checking you out" to see you in a clean, managed manner, and then engage them (hopefully) on your terms. The primary risk is that something that appears on your Facebook Wall might not be consistent with your public brand. (a picture of you partying, etc).

Here's how to register and populate your personal page:

1) **Sign up for Facebook**, and add all of the demographic information that you care to share. Suggestion: Put your birthday, but omit the year. http://www.facebook.com. If you already have a Facebook personal page, then you just need to click *Update Info* to add more data into your profile. Note: Facebook continuously changes their screens and user interface. Some of the screenshots below may not be exactly what you may see online.

2) **Upload images.** When you are in the Timeline view, click on the photos panel to start adding your photos. The two key photos that you must upload are your Cover photo (the big picture of the sunrise, below), and your Profile photo.

From the Photo page, click *Add Photos* to choose specific photos to upload. This is also the way to directly add videos to Facebook.

Note that this page shows Your Albums – photos that you have uploaded – as well as Photos of You – photos that others have uploaded, but are tagged with your name.

The first image that you should upload is a set of product shots, and then (potentially) some professional pictures. You can always add some "fun" personal ones if you like. Make sure that you also upload a "large" picture for the Timeline Cover photo.

Choosing your Cover Photo: From the Timeline page, look for the drop-down menu that says *Add a Cover*. (If you already have a Cover photo, and you want to change it, hover your mouse over the current Cover photo and look for the drop-down menu that says *Change Cover*.)

Choosing a Profile Photo: Hover over the area where the Profile photo should appear, and select *Choose from Photos...* from the drop-down menu. Alternatively, if you are looking at any specific picture, click on the "gear" (settings) drop-down menu at the top-right of the box, and select *Make Profile Picture*.

The Photo application's functionality is tremendously useful. If the event organizer (a "Friend"), took a bunch of pictures of you and uploaded them, the organizer could "tag" you in the picture, and that picture would automatically appear within *your* Photo application. But there is a downside: what if you were on vacation, and a few pictures were taken of you when you were a bit tipsy, or in unflattering clothing? If these made it onto Facebook and were tagged with your name, then there is a huge risk to your professional brand.

Mitigation strategy: either do not use the photo application, use Facebook permissions to lock access to your photo albums, or periodically review your Facebook photos and de-tag yourself from inappropriate pictures. Recommendation: Photos are too strong an opportunity to ignore; keep it open, but periodically review any newly posted photos.

3) Invite Friends: Like LinkedIn, Facebook's utility rises with more and more connections. Click on the panel (below your Cover Photo) labeled *Friends*, in order to get into the Friends area. Click the button *Find Friends*, to get to an area that helps you identify friends from different parts of your life. Hint: use the filters on the left-hand side to see subsets of Facebook's suggestions.

4) Add Bells and Whistles: The basic construction of Facebook is relatively simple: you can extend the functionality of it by adding "apps" to the basic set-up. There are, literally, thousands of apps that can be added – many of them games. Check out the directory at https://www.facebook.com/?sk=apps; scroll down to the tab that says *Friends Using*, to get an idea of what other business-oriented users might find valuable.

How to connect your Blog postings into Facebook:

In the "olden days" of 2009, it was merely a question of adding your blog's feed URL into a dialog box in the Notes application, and Facebook would take care of it all. Then Facebook decided to pull the plug on this functionality, and it is not particularly easy to do this anymore. There are a number of ways to half-way do it; here are three of the alternatives:

a) Use a service like Ping.fm or Hootsuite to push notification of your blog into Facebook. More on these tools later in this Guidebook. (Note that this does not send the entire post, just the headline, a small graphic, and the first few lines.)

b) Use a Facebook App called NetworkedBlogs. Go to the www.NetworkedBlogs.com website, and click on the button to begin. Effectively there are two steps: register your blog on their site, and then connect their site to your Facebook page. The instructions are relatively self-explanatory on their site.

c) Use the Facebook App called RSSGraffiti. This is probably the best approach, as it allows you, all in one place, to auto-publish your Blog feed onto your personal profile, as well as any or all of the Fan pages that you control. To get the App, search for it using the Facebook search box. You will then need to add it to your profile and then authorize it by clicking on the appropriate button on the page.

To connect in your specific feed (or feeds), click the *+Add feed* button (above). You'll be presented with a screen that allows you to identify and customize the feed. Here's what to do:

1) Enter your feed URL.

2) Customize the Source Name. This will let you choose (instead of the system choosing) the source for your feed.

3) Click to generate a preview.

4) Save.

At this point, the feed is configured to appear on your personal Facebook page. You will then need to individually authorize each "Fan Page" that you control so that RSSGraffiti can post there. (We discuss Fan pages in the next section, if you don't yet have one.)

In the left column of the page, there is a list of any Fan pages that you control. Click the grey button to turn on RSSGraffiti for the Fan page; you will then be brought to a page that indicates that you need to give the app more permissions. Click *Click to authorize*, then add your feed to this page, just as you did for your personal page.

Facebook Fan Page

While many people already have individual Facebook pages, you may wish to separate your personal and professional life somewhat - the Facebook "Fan Page" is the mechanism to do this. When your fans interact with your Facebook Fan Page, stories linking to your Fan Page can go to their friends via the News Feed (or in Facebook parlance, the "Wall"). As these friends interact with your Page, the News Feed keeps driving word-of-mouth to an even wider circle of friends.

Other advantages of setting up a Fan Page include:

- the number of "Fans" effectively is unlimited (personal pages and Facebook groups have a limit on how many friends you can have),

- you are able to send messages directly from your Fan page to all of your Fans - without the responses junking up your personal page.

- any application that you can put on a personal page, you can also put on a Fan page. This includes video, photos, and anything else that is of interest.

- You can add some basic branding to your page, beyond a simple photograph.

- Facebook automatically makes an "advertisement" – at no cost to you – and places this ad for your Fan page on your friend's pages.

Click the Facebook Logo to get to your Wall, then on the left edge of the screen click the word *Pages* to open a list of any pages that you are responsible for. Finally, click *Create a Page* to create your Fan page. Note – there is no effective limit on the number of pages that you can create.

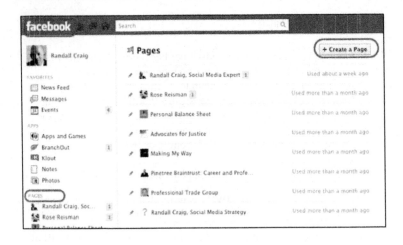

At this point, you will have a choice about your Fan Page's category. Go through each of the categories and subcategories until you find one that makes the most sense. Fill in your page's name in the space provided, select *I agree to Facebook Pages Terms*, then click *create page*. Facebook will then walk you through a step-by-step wizard to help you get yourself set up.

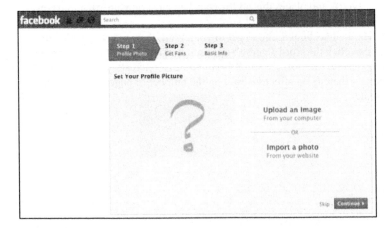

After going through this process, you will be dropped into a special admin-only page for your new Fan page, which gives additional suggestions on getting the most from your efforts.

There are several key things that you must do as soon as possible:

- Claim your page's username. Every page can have a name, which translates into a unique URL for the page. For example, going to www.facebook.com/RandallCraig will go to my Facebook page. To claim your page, follow these steps:

a) Click the *Edit info* button just under the page name, to make changes to the page.

b) On the left-hand navigation area, click on *Basic information*, then click the link in the Username field, to take you to a dialog box that will allow you to choose your Fan page's name/URL.

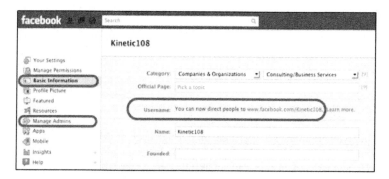

Think carefully about this name, as you will never be able to change it. Once it is selected, you need to confirm it.

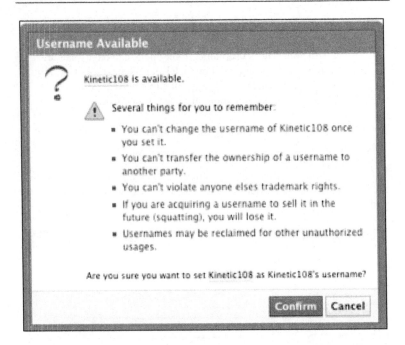

While you are in the settings area, go through each of the other areas, filling it out as you deem appropriate; don't forget to add your website URL, so that the Fan page can act as either an Anchor or Outpost. Another area that you should review more carefully is *Manage Admins*. Unlike personal pages, with Fan pages you can delegate responsibility for managing – *Manage Admins* is where you do this.

The *Resources* area also is also important, in that it is here that you can connect your Facebook Page to your Twitter Account. In general, connecting the two is good, but the question is whether you want Facebook to control the link, or a different Social Media application to do so. We are recommending, later in the book, that you use one "overall" Social Media application (either Ping.fm or Hootsuite.com) to update content across all of your sites, and therefore not to link the two together. If you use Facebook AND a second tool to push data to Twitter, then you will have duplicate entries. If you chose not to use Ping.fm or Hootsuite, just enable the data linking from within Facebook.

The *Apps* area is the gateway to events. Facebook pages provides a quick way to generate interest in your events, and manage the guest list. Don't forget to add an Event Photo.

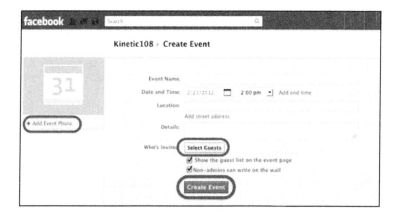

You will definitely want to add videos to your Facebook Fan page. The easiest way to add them is to load the videos directly into Facebook. The Apps area also provides access to the *Video* application to do this. To upload videos, click the *+ Upload* button. (There is also an option to record directly from your webcam, but you would probably prefer to include an already-edited video.)

One of the more interesting things that you can do is allow your Fans to post videos to your page (perhaps as part of a contest?). It means a higher risk and more management time on your part, but it also means greater engagement with your target audience. The default is to allow this; make sure that you turn this off if it is not what you want. Controls for this are in *Video Settings*.

The advantage of using Facebook to hold your videos is that Facebook allows a clip of 20 minutes, while some YouTube accounts are limited to less than this. (It is possible to get a YouTube account with an unlimited time limit.) On the other hand, there is an inconvenience to uploading videos twice: once on YouTube, and the other on Facebook.

Advanced Tip: There are Facebook Applications that you can add to your profile that will pull in your YouTube videos; this simplifies your ongoing maintenance. As well, doing videos this way allows viewership stats to be aggregated in one place: on YouTube.

There are several applications that provide this functionality: Check out *YouTube Gallery for Facebook Pages* at http://budurl.com/YoutubeGallery.

Adding Facebook Apps: There is significant functionality that is available to make your page more powerful, interactive, and customized: just find "the app" that does what you want. Some of these are free, others are paid, and of course, if you wished to, you can develop apps yourself. The challenge is actually finding them. There are two places that can help you explore what is available:

AppBistro: this is a non-Facebook affiliated website (http://budurl.com/appbistro) that provides a curated, organized selection of business-oriented apps.

Within Facebook: Click on the left-hand menu item *Apps*, then scroll down to the page to where it says *Apps and Games*. Method two: if you know the name of an app, or the genre, you can just type it into the Search box at the top of the page. This is how we suggested you add RSSGraffiti, earlier.

At this time, your page is almost complete. You may wish to add photos (click on the *Add Photos* link, and follow a similar process to adding videos), or other media. Photos can be grouped into albums, and people "tagged" within them. Anyone photo that is tagged with a person's name also appears within that person's Facebook account. The magic of this is clear: the more photos that are posted (and tagged), the more event photos that end up in other people's Facebook photo albums. This will drive a surprisingly high number of people back to your Fan page, as they will be interested in seeing many of the other event photos.

Marketing the page

Of course, there are a few things that you should do - notably market the page. Remember, that the more fans you have, the more valuable the page becomes. You can use the page to communicate, on the fly, to all of your fans - and foster a community of interest around your ideas. A few ideas to start:

- Become a Fan of the page yourself. That way, if people find your personal page, they can at least link over to your Fan Page. Go back to the main Fan page and look for a *Like* button near the top of your Fan page, and click it.

- Click the *Share+* button, and share the page with all of your Facebook Friends.

- Include the Fan page URL within your email signature, and anywhere else you advertise your web site.

- Invite your "friends", both of the Facebook type and the real type to become fans of your page. See this related article on how to migrate people from one venue to another: http://budurl.com/smgeography.

- Within your Blog and other content, ensure that there is the Facebook *Like* button. Each time some clicks this, it adds a link to this content within their Facebook page, generating interest both in your original content, as well as you. More on doing this very easily later in the Guidebook, but if you are technically inclined or if you want to see what else you can add onto your site, check out other Facebook plugins at http://budurl.com/fbsocialplugins.

- If you have space on your web site or blog, add a Facebook *Like Box* widget, which pulls Facebook Fan page content into your site, and drives (interested) users back. Example and instructions can be found at http://budurl.com/facebooklikebox.

- Through your existing email database, send invitations to your list encouraging them to become fans and asking them to pass the word out to their friends, colleagues and family.

- Facebook ads: Whether your goal is to drive traffic to your site, advertise a product or service, promote your Facebook Page or encourage users to add your application, Facebook Ads allow you to reach a targeted audience with specific-to-them messages. More on this later in the book.

- Regularly add engaging and useful content. By developing a regular feed of interesting news and discussions, current users will be more inclined to invite their friends to become fans as well.

- Let fans participate in the conversation. By encouraging discussion, you not only benefit from valuable feedback, but also support the development of a community of interest.

Bonus recommendation: If you have an assistant, don't forget to delegate the task of updating your fan page by setting them up as an additional admin for the page. To do this, go to the Admins section in the right-hand column, and click *See All*.

Sometimes, however, you'll want to limit who sees what. Here are two tools to help:

(1) Age Restrictions for Pages: You can restrict your Page to users over age 13, 17, 18, 19, or 21, or the legal drinking age where they live. On your Page's edit page, in the left hand column select *Manage Permissions*.

(2) Targeted Messaging: When you send a message to fans, you can target it by country or language. When sending an update, click on *Public* to expose a drop-down list with several options.

By clicking the *Admin Panel* button on the top right, you'll be able to access a number of additional options, the most important being Facebook Insights. Insights allows you to measure/monitor the reach and engagement of your Fans.

Plaxo

Plaxo (http://www.plaxo.com) began as an annoying site that "managed" your contact list by automatically sending out emails to all of your contacts from time to time, asking them to update their contact information. Then they decided that they would be more liked LinkedIn, with Social Networking functionality, and thankfully this auto-sending of emails stopped. Then in 2011 they stopped the Social Networking, and went back to being an online address book. The strategy with Plaxo is to make it a simple Outpost, and not consider it beyond that.

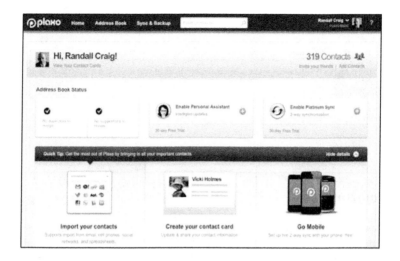

As with all Outposts, go into the *Settings* (under your name in the top-right corner) and turn off most of the email notifications.

MySpace

MySpace is very much like Facebook, but sadly, is now very much a has-been. At its peak in 2008, it recorded 75 million unique monthly visitors, and was valued in the hundreds of millions. In mid 2011, it was sold for $35 million and had a rapidly declining user base. By comparison, in early 2012 Facebook had 845 million monthly visitors.

One of its differentiators has been that it many entertainers and musicians have content within the site – if this is your market, then it may be worthwhile considering it – otherwise, at best, it should be used as an Outpost.

MySpace is trying to reposition itself to a platform for consumption of content, instead of a place for interaction. It is uncertain whether it will survive the next few years.

That being said, if you do wish to invest time here, you can add your blog to your MySpace page. The short form instructions: go to your *Profile*, click *Customize*, Add modules, Edit the content on your profile page and in the modules (including adding your web site's URL and your Blog's RSS feed). And that's it.

Amazon.com

This section is only of interest to you if you have a book that is sold on Amazon.com or certain other international Amazon sites. (This functionality is not currently available everywhere.)

Your Amazon strategy has three parts: (1) Get readers to write positive reviews, (2) Create an author page, and (3) Link your blog to your author page. If your book is wildly successful and sells thousands of copies through Amazon, then you can use this approach to communicate directly to your book's purchasers.

You'll need an Amazon.com username and password, so if you don't have one, go to www.amazon.com and create one. Then go to https://AuthorCentral.Amazon.com, which is the entrypoint for creating a robust author site and begin the process for hooking up your Blog. The instructions for signing up are extremely clear. (You will agree to their terms and conditions, identify which books are yours, and then they will send you a confirmation link.)

Once you've signed up, click on the Author Central *Profile* tab (see below) to begin adding your picture, biography, list of your books, and connect in your blog, Twitter Feed, and events.

For each of the following, click the *edit* link (circled below) to begin the customization process.

Biography: Add a friendly, keyword-rich bio that helps people see beyond your professional expertise.

Blogs: You will need your blog's RSS feed URL; note that Amazon will not import old posts, only new ones. Having your blog appear here is a great way to drive traffic from interested Amazon shoppers back to your main site. And it also allows prospective purchasers to sample how you think.

Events: Another way to publicize any events that you are doing. Each event is keyed to one of your books.

Author Page URL: This is a way for you to claim a unique, direct URL for your author page. Once it is set, it cannot ever be changed, so consider what you choose carefully. (My Amazon.com URL is http://www.amazon.com/author/randallcraig. As there are other published authors with my name, claiming this early was pretty important.)

Video: Sadly, Amazon does not allow video embeds from other sites (eg from YouTube); it only accepts short videos that you upload directly from your desktop. Video is very powerful, but it needs to be produced as professionally as your book... otherwise your brand will suffer.

Twitter: Amazon will display your latest Tweet, along with your Twitter @name, directly on your author profile. Again, like your blog, this is another channel to connect with readers and prospective purchasers.

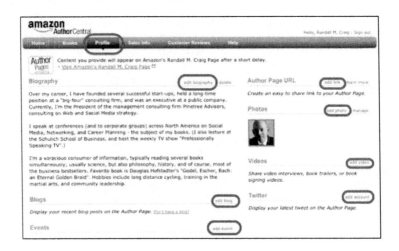

After the Profile information is added, you will need to add and/or modify the books that are connected to your profile. This can be done through the *Books* menu item at the top of the page.

The most powerful part of Author Central is that you can change the content that is displayed on the Amazon listing for your book – and add more information that the publisher was too lazy to do for you. In the *Books* section of the site, click on one of your books to begin the review and editing process.

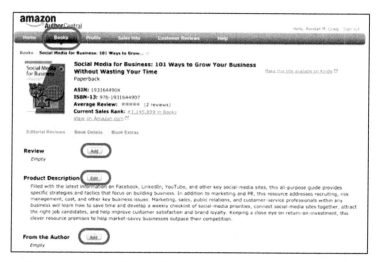

At this point you can click on the various *Add* and *Edit* buttons to make whatever changes you see are necessary. Don't forget that you can also go into the Book Details (and Book Extras) to do more customization. Interestingly, Amazon has purchase Shelfari.com, which is a public web site that allows people to add information about their favorite books. Amazon pulls Shelfari data into their site, and displays this on your book's page. As you have a unique insight into your book – and you want to ensure that your positive-spin content appears on Amazon – you should spend the time on Shelfari to enter your data there.

Here is how a completed Amazon Author Page can look:

Wikipedia

Wikipedia is a user-written and user-edited online encyclopedia. If you are in it, then you can be found if someone searches for you – or for your area of expertise. The Wikipedia strategy involves three activities: Adding to existing articles (including adding your books as references, if appropriate), writing reference articles in your area of expertise, if they don't already exist (most do), and creating a personal biographical page.

We recommend that you perform a search from time to time, to check how others may have quoted you, but editing and creating articles is a fairly technical (and time-consuming) process that you might wish to consider only AFTER doing all of the other activities within this guidebook.

To register, you need to go through several pages. First, go to the http://www.wikipedia.org main home page, and click on the *English* (or other language, as appropriate) link.

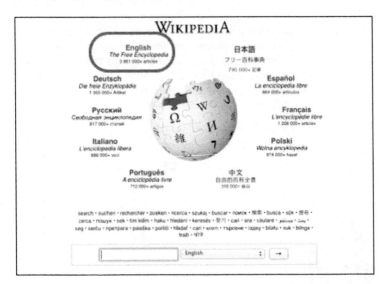

Then, click on the *Log in /create account* link, in the top-right corner.

Finally, create your account by clicking on *Create one*.

If you are thinking of creating/editing pages, here are some useful links to get you started:

- General help index page: http://en.wikipedia.org/wiki/Help:Contents

- To learn how to create your first article:
  http://en.wikipedia.org/wiki/Wikipedia:Your_first_article

Squidoo

Squidoo is an interesting site, in that it allows you to create special-interest pages (called *Lenses*) that highlight particular topics. We recommend that you create one for each sub-area of your expertise. Not only will the cross-links help your search engine ranking, but these pages serve as additional Outposts for you. Go to http://www.squidoo.com to start, and click *Join for free* to begin.

Once you have completed the registration process (or when you sign in later), you can click on the top of the page to start your first lens

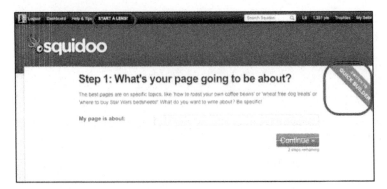

There are two ways to create a lens – either with the screen-by-screen wizard (shown above), or with the "quick-builder", that lets you fill out all of the information on one page, all at once. The quick builder is faster, but has less on-screen help. Whichever your preference, there are two steps to building a lens: first, choose the modules that will be on the page, and second, fill the modules with text, pictures, videos, links, etc.

After this process, you will be brought to a page (your "Workshop") where you can fill in more details by clicking the *Edit* button throughout the page. Note that many of the modules on the page are irrelevant, and clicking the *X* button to the right of the *Edit* button will remove the undesired section.

Without a question, you will want to add your Blog, YouTube videos, as well as a branding image and description. For even more customization, look through the *Workshop Tools* area. Once you're finished, click *Publish* at the top of the page

Advanced user note: Squidoo has dozens of modules that can be added to your lenses. As you go through the site, you will see that Squidoo can pull in your Blog, Twitter, Flickr photos, YouTube videos, and a ton of other content from elsewhere. While it is tempting to link all of these up, remember that each Squidoo lens is really an Outpost site – not an Anchor. If you post too much here, users and potential members may never find their way to your organization's Anchor sites. Yet, if your organization posts too little, then the lens has little value, and it is unlikely to be found.

As you create each lens, remember to click *Publish* to ensure that the site moves from *Work in Process* (WIP) status, to live status. WIP status means it isn't published on the web. Currently, Squidoo has the annoying habit of downgrading your lenses to WIP status whenever there have been no changes on your page, which means that you will need to calendarize to go in, make a minor change, and then republish. (You may wish to check every two-three months.) Furthermore, Squidoo programmatically reviews each lens when you publish it; if it appears that there is little content, it will still let you publish it, but the lens will not be indexed – which removes it's value as an Outpost completely.

You can create as many lenses as you wish: the more single-purpose they are, the more powerful they will be in attracting relevant users.

Before you leave Squidoo, click on *My Settings (or Settings – they go to the same place)*, and add any information that you would like, paying particular attention to the web site and blog addresses that you add.

An example of a minimalist completed page can be found at www.Squidoo.com/randallcraig.

Yahoo Answers, Askville, and other How-to sites.

You can spend hours, every day, trying to answer the flood of questions on these How-to sites. As an expert, it is an important strategic question as to how much time you spend asking questions and making yourself "known".

My recommendation is to spend time answering questions only if your target market "hangs out" there. For example, if you are a member of a specialized LinkedIn group, you may get a better return answering questions there, than, say, Yahoo Answers (http://answers.yahoo.com) or Askville (http://askville.amazon.com). One other possibility: instead of committing ongoing time to answering questions, only answer 3-5 questions in each area, so that if someone searches for your name, at least you would appear in the results.

As in all Outposts, after registering, *Edit your profile* to ensure that your web addresses are entered (and marketing emails are turned off.)

It also makes sense to choose the questions that you answer, based on your ability to repurpose your answer, either in your Blog, or in some other writing project that you are working on.

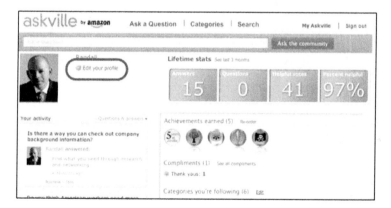

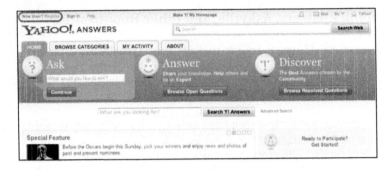

Xing

Xing (http://www.xing.com) works very similar to LinkedIn, and should be handled as an Outpost site. This social network seems more focused on Europe than North America; interestingly, they have an ambassador program that seeks to develop real-world networking events in different geographies.

To get to your profile and add your details, click on the small picture in the top left corner to get to your profile page, then continue scrolling down the page to add/change content, clicking *Edit* your data. Adjust system-wide settings icon on the far right.

Google

Google has a number of free applications, including Gmail (email services), AdWords (advertising), Docs (shared word processing/spreadsheets/presentation tools), Analytics (web site usage tracking), Google+, and many, many more. Chances are that you use at least one of these services – if you do, then you have a Google account. If not, then you can sign up for free, by clicking the *Sign in* link on the top right-hand corner of the Google home page.

One of the most powerful new features from Google is their Google+ Social Network. If you are not on it yet, you should be, for a host of reasons:

- Google+ has a direct influence on Google's search results – including where you are positioned.

- Google+ is currently not easily connectable to other Social Networks – which means that much of the content that appears is unique.

- It is a growing Social Media site, and thus represents another channel for you to connect with your target audience.

- There is some interesting functionality that exists only here.

- Google+ forms the center of your online identity in the Google world, and will likely be integrated into more and more of the Google products.

- Google is likely to support it and grow it significantly, as it is their most likely competitive defense against Facebook.

Despite these compelling reasons, at the time of writing Google+ has not developed the traction of a Facebook or LinkedIn: the jury is out whether it ultimately will be successful. That being said, Google is just too important to ignore, and a small investment of your time now will likely pay off over time.

To begin with Google+, either click on the top-right *+You*, or click *Join Google+* in the top right-hand drop-down under your name.

While the screen might look slightly different, the next step is to create a public Google profile, and "upgrade" yourself into the Google+ world. Fill in your name, select your gender, add a picture, and the click *Upgrade*.

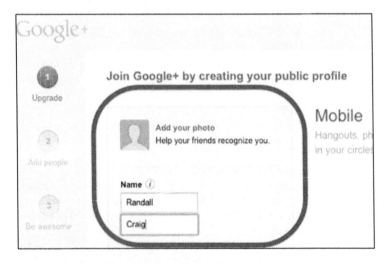

After registering with Google+, the system will ask you to connect people into your "Circles", by reading in people from other web sources. Circles are how you control who sees what: they are groupings of people. Google provides some "standard" circles, including Friends, Family, Acquaintances, Following. Some other ideas for circle names might include Association members, Staff, Clients, Alumni, No relationship, etc. Choose whatever circle names make sense to you.

Finally, Google+ will ask you to fill out more personal information, in order to help others find you. To fill out other settings, you will need to go to two different places. For account-related information, including communications preferences, click on the *settings* button on the right hand column of the main page.

For personal profile information, including links to your other Social Media profiles, click the Profile icon (left column), and then click the large *Edit Profile* button, also on the right.

Like LinkedIn or Facebook, Google+ is not a one-trick pony: there is significant functionality within it. Here are a few examples, and how you might consider using the tool:

1) Critical is adding more people to your circles. Only when you can reach out and connect can you interact. Click on the Circles icon, which is located in the left column to get to the page where you can add people. Simply search for potential connections, and "follow" them by dragging their image to a circle, further down the page. People can be in as many circles as is appropriate.

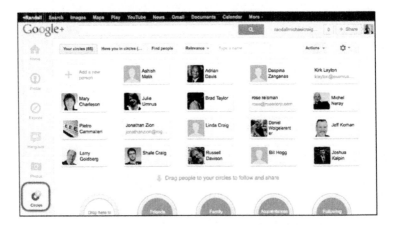

2) Communicate to your circles: Google+'s version of Facebook's *Like* button is their *+1* button. Whenever you click on a +1 anywhere on the web, this is sent to your Google+ page for your circle's consumption. Another way to communicate is to add a comment (or link, or picture) from your own Google+ page.

3) Comment on your connection's posts.

4) Start a *Hangout* with one of your circles. A hangout is a virtual space where you can share and collaborate. From a practical perspective, you can chat, watch a YouTube video together, and share your screen, all while each person's webcam is on. Think of it as cheap-and-effective teleconferencing.

Like Facebook Pages, Google+ uses the concept of "corporate" pages that can be administered separately from your personal page. And like Facebook, you first need to create your personal page before you can create the corporate page. (And also like Facebook, you can delegate responsibility for this page to an administrator.) Look for a link in the bottom-right corner that says *Create a Google+ Page*.

Just because you can create one, though, doesn't mean that you should. The management and maintenance time required to keep up the page, especially in the early days of the tool, can be onerous. (Our opinion: we believe that it is important to have a corporate page on Google+, as it eventually will take off; we just have a difficult time justifying the time investment.)

Interestingly, these Profiles are directly searchable using the following special URL: http://www.google.com/profiles?q=. They are also searchable – with a better interface - directly from within Google+.

Note: Google profiles are highly integrated into the Google search algorithm. Not only does your profile show up in search results, but your profile and connections now influence your search results.

Google Places

One of the more interesting aspects of Google Maps is that you are able to have your physical location appear within Google Maps. This provides enhanced information for those searching for you, or searching within a certain geography. To begin the process, go to http://maps.google.com, and then click on *Put your business on Google Maps*.

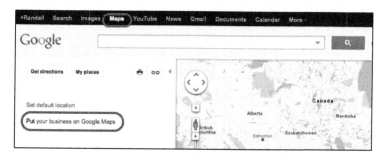

There are detailed instructions on the screens that follow, taking care to also enter your web site address, so that this entry can function as an Outpost. (To begin, click *+Add*

another business, and begin filling out the forms with your organization's details.)

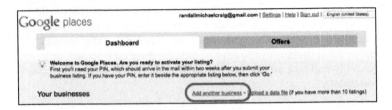

To verify that you indeed have a business at that address, they will send you a postcard through traditional mail, containing a special PIN code and URL. Go to the Places web site, and enter the PIN, and your business location will be shown within Google Maps. (And the business location entry will also appear within the regular Google search results.)

One interesting additional twist from Google Places is the ability to add an "offer" (eg coupon) to your web listing. If you have product, consider adding this here, with a coupon code and a shortened URL (eg bitly.com) address for your online store. Click on the right-hand tab – *Offers* – to find out more.

Yahoo

Yahoo Profiles: Using a process similar to Google's, we recommend that you create a Yahoo Profile with your basic contact information. In addition, Yahoo is hoping to develop a Social Networking component, with "connections". We recommend that your Yahoo profile be handled as an Outpost site. This means accepting anyone who asks you to be a connection, but not actively soliciting them.

To get a Yahoo profile, you will need to sign up for *Yahoo Mail*, if you haven't done so. You will not use this email address; it is only a required step in order to have a Yahoo member profile.

After you have done this, go to the Profiles page (http://profiles.yahoo.com) to begin the Profile creation process, entering the basic demographic information. There is an edit profile button on the profile page for you to make additional changes.

Unlike most identity sites, there is no simple "bio" that you can cut-and-paste existing text, but instead, Yahoo requires you to fill out specific fields with information. Since each of these fields has a maximum character count, you may have to shoe-horn in your bio by cutting it up into shorter bits.

Once you have completed the basic profile build-out, you can link this profile to Facebook and Twitter. If you wish to make the connection, click on the *Settings Gear* in the right hand area of your profile.

On the *Settings* page in the *Linked Accounts* section, click the icons to link your Twitter account and your Facebook page.

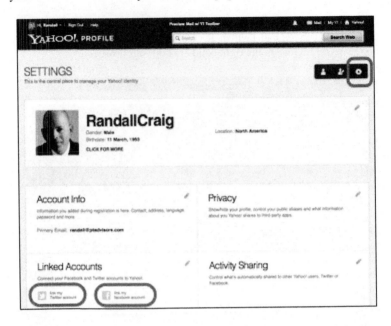

Once you've clicked the various authorize pop-up windows, the linked accounts will be connected. Interestingly, Yahoo also owns Flickr, the relatively successful photo-sharing site. Why they haven't connected it to the profiles defies imagination.

Yahoo had been trying to move into the Social Networking space, with a product called *Yahoo! Pulse*, but they have recently turned this off completely, in favor of the simplified, non-social profiles. It bears watching if they will add this back, perhaps under a different name.

Note: Yahoo, as well as several other news portals, offer a way to "connect" your Facebook profile (see Yahoo! Shine for an example). This represents a serious risk, as every article that you read is displayed on your Facebook wall for others to see... and judge you on.

Pinterest

Pinterest calls itself an online pinboard, where you can "pin" graphics that you find around the web, and where others can like, comment, and repin on their own Pinterest pages.

Pinterest is highly viral, in that anything that you "pin" can be seen on Facebook and Twitter, generating more views, comments, likes, and affinity for you and your brand. Because of this, it is relatively important for you to consider carefully what you pin on your boards: you don't want your brand "tugged" in the wrong direction.

There are two key activities that you should do to use this tool effectively, beyond signing up at www.Pinterest.com.

1) Click *Edit Profile*, both to fill in your basic information and connect your web site, Twitter and Facebook accounts.

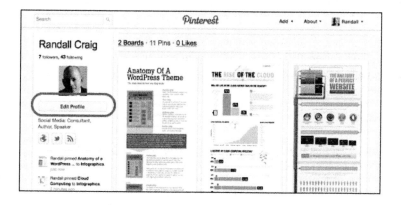

2) Add the *Pin It* button to your browser's bookmarks/favorites, so that you can easily pin content that you see on the web to your Pinterest page.

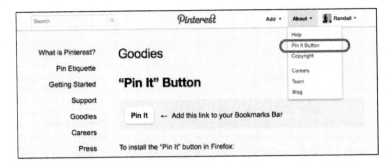

There is a small amount of controversy surrounding Pinterest, in the area of intellectual property. Since Pinterest actually copies content into the site (eg onto one of your boards), there is a question of rights and liabilities. The current terms and conditions state that by using Pinterest, you have full rights to post whatever you post, and that you give Pinterest the right to repurpose this content howsoever they choose. The problem is that most people do NOT have rights to the content they pin: if you use the platform, then you may put yourself at risk.

Furthermore, as an expert who may have content posted online, you should be aware that others may Pin your content without your permission or approval. Depending on your strategy, this may or may not be a good thing.

eBay

Remember that your clients (and others) may look for you just about anywhere, including on sites such as eBay. Assuming you have registered on eBay, click through to your *My eBay* page from the top right links. Then click your name, to display your *My World* Profile.

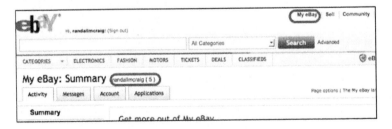

From this page, you can add/change your picture, bio, add various other types of content, change the layout, etc. Note: If you wish to keep your eBay transactions private, consider opening (and using) a second account using a pseudonym.

As an Outpost site, we don't see much value in spending much time on eBay, other than putting in the most basic of information.

Staking your territory

Depending on your industry or specialization, you may need to set up profile pages on various other social media sites too. Before you spend too much time, though, consider whether you should set up an Anchor site - like LinkedIn or Facebook - or whether you should set up an Outpost - like Plaxo or others. There are over 500+ social networking and identity sites on the internet. Developing a profile on each of them, let alone keeping them current, is time-consuming.

On the other hand, if someone shares your name, you might wish to register on as many social networking sites as you can find, if only to prevent that someone from taking your username before you do. Thankfully, checking is relatively easily done. The following web site allows you to check if your username is taken yet, or not, across dozens of web sites, all at once: http://knowem.com. If this site is not working, then an alternative that does the same thing is http://www.usernamez.com.

The vast majority of these sites are not directly relevant, except for their pre-emptive value. Most are not social networking sites, but portals (eg Yahoo), photo-sharing sites (Flickr), or Web Applications (eg Picasa, Pandora.). (If you don't have a Blog, you might look at Wordpress, Typepad, or Blogger, though.)

If you have a lot of time on your hands, or have an intern who isn't too busy, you can register yourself on each of these, setting each site up as a far-away outpost. (Knowem.com also has a premium version that does this for you, at a relatively low cost.)

Chapter Four: Claiming your profiles before others do

Aggregator sites are ones that continuously browse through the entire internet, collecting every reference to your name, and then automatically creating a "profile" of you. The problem, however, is that much of the data on these aggregated pages is merely for people who have the same name as you.

These sites generally allow you to *claim* the page as your own – something that is critically important for you to do, for two reasons:
* To prevent someone else from claiming your page; (eg, to prevent identity theft.)
* To remove the incorrect references; (clients and prospects, after all, will find these pages.)

Four key aggregator sites include Squidoo, ZoomInfo, Spoke, and Data.com (formerly known as Jigsaw). Unfortunately, there are a growing number of these sites; at the end of the chapter we've listed a few more.

ZoomInfo

ZoomInfo's business model is to sell [fairly expensive] access to sales professionals who are looking for prospects, and to recruiters who are looking for hidden job candidates.

To begin the claiming process, go to www.Zoominfo.com and search for your name. In the screen shot below, notice that there are a lot of Randall Craig's and Randy Craig's – yet only a few of them are me. What would happen if any of those other Randall's "claimed" *my* page?

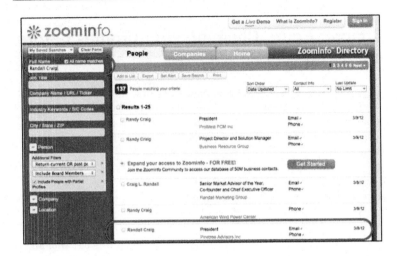

From these search results, click on the first name that appears to be yours. Look at the information on the page, and click through to the online sources; the example below shows that the profile was created using one web reference. If the profile is yours, then you will want to "claim" it. To do this, you will need to sign in (or register, if you haven't yet done so), and then click the *Claim This Profile* link.

After claiming the page, you will want to update your profile to show your background, and to link back to your Anchor Sites. To make changes, click on *My Account* in the top-right corner.

The page below is "claimed", and has been cleaned up.

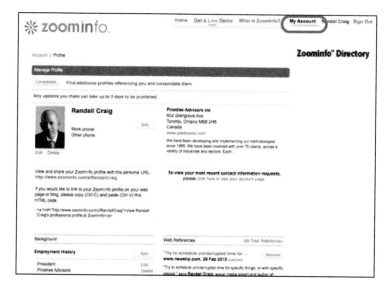

Once this is done for the first reference to your name, then repeat the process for all of the others. When you click the *Claim this Profile* button, a window will open asking you if you want to make the selected profile your profile: this is NOT what happens - the system actually MERGES this profile with your existing one.

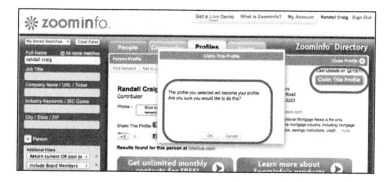

After the merger, clean up "extra" job listings etc from your profile. Make sure that the dates match the dates shown in your other profile sites. In the case below, I would choose to delete this extra Employment History item, as it is not really Employment History – it's an article that I wrote.

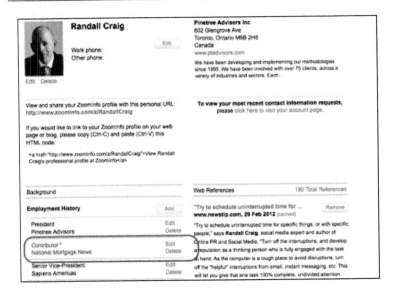

ZoomInfo also allows you to claim your company page. You can search for your company name by clicking on the appropriate tab on the top of the page, and following a similar process for claiming as you did when you claimed your personal page. Once you have edited the company page, if you ever want to re-edit it, then click on the *My Account* link at the very top-right corner of the page, and then click on the *Company Profile* link in the left hand navigation.

Risk: Beyond the issue of the unclaimed profiles, Zoominfo.com has another service that is also a major area of risk. Their *Zoominfo Community Edition* is a plug-in that attaches to Outlook, that provides access to some 50 million contacts. Not bad, except that the currency that you pay for these contacts... is allowing everyone else access to yours. Recommendation: don't ever do this.

Spoke

Spoke is very similar to ZoomInfo, both in its business model, and how to claim your profile. To begin, go to http://www.spoke.com, and search for your name.

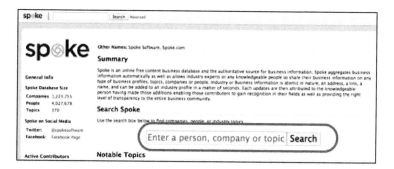

When you find the name, fill in the blanks, and then click *This is Me*. If you haven't logged in or registered yet, you will be asked to do so first.

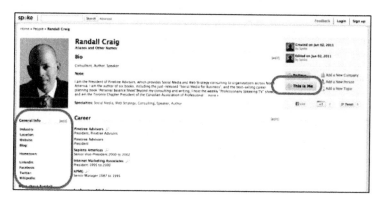

One note on Spoke: at the time of writing, you were only able to claim your Personal page, not your Company page.

Data.com (formerly Jigsaw)

Data.com, formerly www.Jigsaw.com, is a sales-oriented contact-sharing website owned by the giant CRM platform, SalesForce.com. Go to www.Jigsaw.com to directly access the services for individuals. Users gain points for uploading their contacts, which they can then "spend" on gaining access to other's contact details. This system provides a built-in incentive for people to add your information online. Or, for as little as $21/month, you can access the entire database, but only up to a set number of contacts each year. Given the connection to Salesforce.com, expect any data in this database to be used by any number of companies or people within the Salesforce.com ecosystem.

Jigsaw is actually quite confusing, in that as a member you have a username, and because you may or may not be listed in their contact database, you may also have a "business card". Here is what you need to do:

1) Make sure that any business cards are updated, and do not contain incorrect data.

2) Set up a notification so that if anyone else changes your business cards, you are notified.

3) Finally, you may wish to update your company information.

The first step is to search for your name on the site, then register to update your name. (You can register first, then search for your name, if you prefer.)

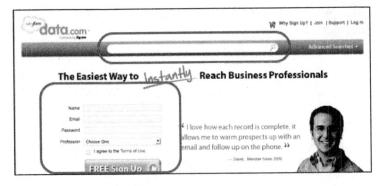

On the resulting screen, click on the name of the person (eg yourself) that you want to update, and make any appropriate changes.

To set up an email notification if someone changed your business card, click on the link in the footer of the page, entitled *Are you in data.com?* This will bring you to a different search page, where you can search business cards by email address. If you are in the database, you will then be asked to type in a CAPTCHA code, after which the system will send an email to your address. Clicking on the link within that address will bring you to a page that is not accessible elsewhere within the system, where you can review the business card's contact information, *and also set a notification if ANYONE changes your data.*

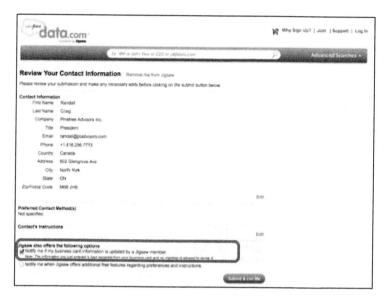

After you have created your account, updated any business cards, and set the change notifications, you should also add your company. This can be done through the *Companies* drop-down menu. Suggestion: first search for the company, and only if it doesn't exist, then add it.

Filed by Author

This site (www.filedby.com) has created pages for over 3 million authors. (The criteria is that your book has an ISBN number, and is published in the United States or Canada.) There is no cost to claim your "basic" page, fill it with appropriate "Outpost" content, and then link it to your main sites.

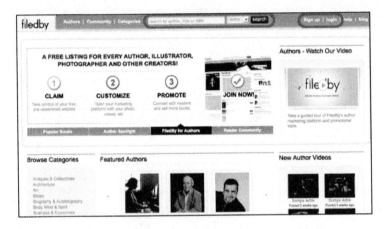

SpeakerMix.com

Designed for working speakers, this site began as a Wiki (it still is, actually), where anyone could update information on themselves, by first registering and then "claiming" their profile. If your profile doesn't exist, then you can add it by clicking on the link at the bottom of the page.

To edit your profile, click *Edit* near the top-right corner. This site has the potential to be almost a "Super Outpost", given all of the potential links and references that it can hold.

Goodreads.com

www.Goodreads.com is a site for readers to add their favorite books, recommend others, and discover yet others. If you have books, then registering on this site in their (free) author program gives you the ability to tap into this community, and make it your own. To get into their author program, first register as a regular user, then find your books. When you do, click on the link *Is this you?* and follow the instructions. (Your account will be upgraded to Author, then giving you an ability to customize your online presence within the site.)

About.me

This site creates a one-page billboard of you. My personal about.me page is accessible at http://about.me/randallcraig, which should give you a clue about the risk to you: what if someone with the same name – or a troublemaker – claimed this address for themselves?

www.Twylah.com

Twylah.com is a site that automatically creates a "site" for your Tweets, grouped by hashtag. Very clever, and well-designed. Implemented well, it should drive additional Twitter traffic, or act as a very special-purpose microsite.

Other sites

Unfortunately, the number of "aggregator" sites is growing, and growing quickly. While most will not ever become successful – or even be seen by most people – it is important to recognize the risk that these sites represent, and be quick to claim them when you see them. Even Google and Bing, with their local search, allows you to "Add or Edit your Business" - which others can do to your detriment.

Here are a few of the others:

- www.wink.com (Search for yourself, and/or Register by clicking on "Take Charge now...")

- www.lead411.com/profilepromote (Add both yourself and your company, if it's not already there.)

- www.reputation.com (This is another "reputation monitor" company that searches for you online and by paying them a fee, they will attempt to repair/fix it if there are problems. Claiming/creating your profile is almost too easy.)

- www.truerep.com (This is a front-end for the intelius.com people, one of the bigger data aggregators; to claim your profile, you need to "verify" your identity, which means putting in your US address: clearly a problem for people who are not American.)

- www.radaris.com (Can register, but cannot currently "Claim" a profile of your own.)

- www.pipl.com (An interesting aggregator site to look at because of it's depth, but does not allow profiles to be claimed.)

- www.peekyou.com (At one time allowed you to claim your profile, but seemingly has removed this capability.)

- www.WikiDomo.com (A guide for your community, maintained by the community.

- Depending on your industry, there may be some industry-specific profiles that you should claim. For example, if you are a lawyer, claim your profile on www.avvo.com and www.justia.com. If you are a local food/farmer in New York, claim your profile on www.whatisfresh.com. Sadly – or fortunately – there are no shortage of sites that now offer this "helpful" ~~identity theft~~ customer service.

- While most professionals typically are not in the "walk-in" business, there are a number of local listings sites (beyond Google and Bing) that it makes sense to review and register/claim your page on. At worst, each registration is another Outpost. At best, it reduces the risk of identity theft:

  - http://www.ibegin.com (Data source for other websites)

  - http://www.macraesbluebook.com (Manufacturing/industrial suppliers; hint: register under "training services")

  - http://www.manta.com (Small business listings)

  - http://www.radiatelocal.com (Local business listings)

  - www.jayde.com (Business directory)

  - www.hotfrog.com (Business directory)

  - www.kudzu.com (Find a pro site)

  - www.matchpoint.com (Business search site.)

  - www.openlist.com (Local review site)

  - www.spotlikes.com (recommendation engine for businesses)

  - www.weblocal.ca (business listings)

  - www.yellowbot.com (Review and "tagging" site)

  - www.yelp.com (major site: location-based business reviews)

You may wish to look at www.GetListed.org (US/UK/Canada only), as a way to quickly see where and how your company is listed on a few of the major sites.

Finally, there is no shortage of data brokers who aggregate content, and then (sometimes) allow you to register (pipl.com and radaris.com, from above, are examples). This site (http://www.privacyrights.org/online-information-brokers-list) contains a huge list of providers. Remember that the goal is not necessarily to remove yourself from each of these broker sites, but rather to ensure that the data is correct, add links to your anchors and main site, and if possible, claim the site profiles so that no one else can do so.

Chapter Five: Wire the sites together

Videos

Add to main web site

While it is possible to host your Video on your own web site, you might prefer to host it on YouTube, then installing a YouTube "widget" (a few lines of HTML code) on your site to play the video there. The advantages of this include:

- There are no bandwidth charges from YouTube for playing your video

- You only need upload your video in one place, not several.

- Viewer statistics are compiled in one place

Disadvantages include:

- You may not want related videos, or other YouTube content, to appear within the YouTube window, after yours has finished playing.

- Some organizations will actually filter out YouTube content at their firewall, which means that your web pages will have "blank" sections in them wherever YouTube was supposed to appear. Note: some organizations filter ALL video content, not just YouTube hosted content.

How to embed your video within your web site: First go to that video on YouTube.

Click on the button just below the video that says *Share*, then decide how you would like to share the video.

If you just want to link to the YouTube video page itself, copy out the link. YouTube has recently begun using their own link shortener (youtu.be) for this. Here is an example:

http://youtu.be/yRXGZQ5OU2g

If you want to share it on Facebook, Twitter, Google+, or others, then click the appropriate direct button. You will need to set this up beforehand: see below for how to do this.

If you want to embed the video itself within another web page (or within your blog), then click the *Embed* button, and copy out the HTML snippet. YouTube has two versions of the embed code. The newer one is shorter, and looks like this:

```
<iframe width="560" height="315"
src=http://www.youtube.com/embed/yRXGZQ5OU2g
frameborder="0" allowfullscreen></iframe>
```

Some websites do not recognize this newer embed code, and require you to use the older one. To get the older one, just click one of the options underneath ("Use old embed code"). Here's what it looks like:

```
<object width="560" height="315"><param name="movie"
value="http://www.youtube.com/v/yRXGZQ5OU2g?version=3&a
mp;hl=en_US"></param><param name="allowFullScreen"
value="true"></param><param name="allowscriptaccess"
value="always"></param><embed
src="http://www.youtube.com/v/yRXGZQ5OU2g?version=3&amp
;hl=en_US" type="application/x-shockwave-flash"
width="560" height="315" allowscriptaccess="always"
allowfullscreen="true"></embed></object>
```

Paste this into your web site's authoring tool, or give this to your webmaster to add. Marketing Note: YouTube automatically suggests other videos when yours is finished. Since you don't ever want this to happen – they may suggest either a competitor, or an opponent's video - you must deselect *Show suggested videos when the video finishes.* This will add "<u>**?rel=0**</u>" into the embed code for you automatically. Here is how the newer embed code will look:

```
<iframe width="560" height="315"
src=http://www.youtube.com/embed/yRXGZQ5OU2g?rel=0
frameborder="0" allowfullscreen></iframe>
```

There is one example of a site, from a PR company, that either doesn't know about this, or was sloppy. After their video pitch for their (very interesting) journalist-to-expert matching service, the YouTube window filled up with unrelated videos: pets, abusive relationships, and so on.

Add to your Blog

At one time, YouTube could auto-push (eg syndicate) new videos to your blog. Now, if you want to have the videos in your blog, you will need to either manually add them into your blog, or use a plug-in within your blog to accomplish this for you.

Add to Facebook and Twitter

To have this happen automatically, you will need to set this up beforehand. In the top-right corner, click on your account name in order to expose the menu, then click on *Settings*. In the left-hand navigation menus, click *Sharing*, and then finally choose how you want to share any new videos. Generally, you will want to connect your Twitter and Facebook accounts, and possibly others (such as Orkut) if you are on them. Once you are finished, click the *Save Changes* button on the bottom of the screen.

Connect your Blogs to other sites.

In addition to connecting your Blog to your social networking and identity sites (eg LinkedIn, Amazon, and Facebook). There are a number of "blog aggregator" sites that will take your Blog's feed, repackage it, and then make it available to others. The benefit of this means that your blog will appear in many additional places, with the resulting important side-benefit of increased search engine rankings.

Google FeedBurner

This completely free service has grown rather substantially, and is now owned by Google. To sign up, go to http://feedburner.google.com, and go through the registration process. In order to access the functionality, you will need a Google Account. The first step is to claim your feeds.

The first step is to claim your feeds – relatively straightforward.

There are a ton of tracking and other tools that you might want to explore within FeedBurner, but there is one that is critically important: PingShot.

Once you've signed in, click on the *Publicize* tab, and choose *PingShot* from the left hand menu. Whenever FeedBurner receives your Blog posting, PingShot will then tell ("Ping") all of the chosen services about your new post, which will then result in each service getting that post.

Don't forget to click *Activate*:

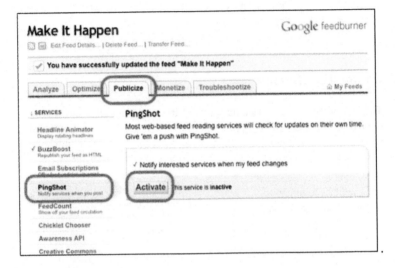

Technorati

This site, at http://www.technorati.com, is one of the leading blog aggregators on the internet. Literally, it takes in feeds from millions of blogs, categorizes them, organizes them into a nifty directory, and lets the content be searchable. Like other social network sites, it also has a rating component, allowing more popular posts to receive higher priority.

Sign up by clicking *Join* in the top right corner, and then filling in the registration information. Remember that since this is an Outpost site, you should include links to your main sites within the bio.

After doing this, you will be required to validate your identity by clicking on a link that they send to you via email. When you click on this, you will be taken to a page where you can type in your Blog's feed URL, and begin the "claim" process. (The claim process allows you to prove that you are, indeed, the blog's owner.)

You then have the opportunity to categorize your blog, add tags/keywords, and other identifying meta data.

The claim process is relatively simple: Technorati will send you an email with a code in it (they call it a *Token*), and you will need to make a blog post that includes that code. After you do so, click on the "*Check Claim*" button within your Technorati profile page, and it will go to your site to verify that you indeed were able to add the code onto your page. Once this is done (and Technorati says that the claim is verified), you can then delete the page with the code on it.

At this point, your blog will be "awaiting final review". Usually it will move from this stage to "Live" within a few days.

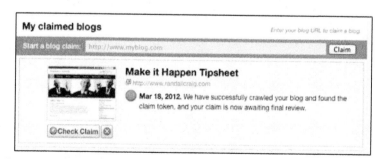

Social Bookmarking

There are a number of sites on the internet where people can "save" bookmarks for sites, blog entries, and other bits of content. Then, these social bookmarking sites categorize the entries, make them searchable, and allow their users to vote on the popularity of the entry. Four of the most well-known social bookmarking sites are Reddit (http://www.reddit.com), Digg (http://www.digg.com), Stumbleupon (http://www.stumbleupon.com), and Delicious (http://del.icio.us). There are a number of others as well (Technorati, discussed earlier, has a social bookmarking component). You may have seen these sites through the almost ubiquitous icons that appear at the bottom of many blog entries or web pages, asking if you want to share the page.

The more other people are likely to share (and therefore propagate) your content, the better your exposure will be. While you may need to enlist the help of your webmaster, ask them to install either addthis (http://www.addthis.com) or sharethis (http://www.sharethis.com) to your blog and to your web site. Here is a graphic of the sharethis pop-up menu, showing all of the various social bookmarking sites:

Whenever someone clicks on one of the social bookmarking links, the current page's URL is sent/posted to that site – resulting in even more exposure for you.

Newsletters

It takes a significant amount of time to write, edit, and finally send your email newsletters (*ezines*) to your subscribers. There are two things that you should do to leverage this effort: repurpose your ezine articles onto free article web sites, and repurpose this same content into your blog.

The two key problems with ezines are email deliverability and inbox overload. If your email isn't stopped as spam, then often your readers just don't get a chance to read them because they arrive along with so many other "important" emails.

There is only one sure way to ensure that your ezine is on your subscribers' must-read list: your content must be timely, relevant, well-written, and of the highest possible value. If this is true, then your subscribers will make sure that it doesn't get caught by the spam filters – and they will read it immediately when it comes in.

Blog

As you went to the trouble of writing your newsletter, there is no reason why you shouldn't get as much mileage out of it as possible: re-purpose your articles as blog postings. While your current readership might not all subscribe to your blog, others will, and this is a key way to mitigate the deliverability problem. And it's a great way to keep your blog up-to-date as well.

Article Marketing

While *article marketing* is not online PR, it is an important way to get your message out, establish yourself as an expert in your area, and at the same time get a search engine ranking benefit. (The SEO benefit of article marketing has been vastly reduced, however, as Google now penalizes duplicate copies of substantially similar articles.)

If the articles within your ezines are long enough to stand on their own, you may wish to post them on the various free (or paid) article-posting web sites that exist. Other people will then either read your articles on those sites directly, or download them and post your articles on their own sites. Note though, by participating in certain of these sites, you are essentially giving others perpetual rights to reprint/republish your content, without any payment to you. Some do's and don'ts:

- Read the fine print on each site to know exactly what rights you are giving away. If you are hoping to use your articles within an upcoming book, traditional publishers may require that all rights be signed over to them – something that might be impossible if your articles are posted rights-free online. At the same time, look to avoid fine print that requires that your article appear exclusively on one site, and not on any other free article sites.

- At the bottom of your article, after the article itself, embed a one sentence mini-bio of yourself. Include your name, title, company name, expertise, Twitter name, and web site address. Do not include an email address, as spammers will harvest this and send you an un-ending stream of spam.

- Put your name under the title. (eg "By Randall Craig") Better yet, include key words that would be indexed by Google. (eg "By Randall Craig, Social Media Expert")

- Use a headline that speaks to the problem that you are solving, but that has a twist in it that catches the readers' attention.

- Make sure that your first paragraph also catches their attention. If it doesn't, they won't read further – and you'll not have an opportunity to credentialize yourself.

Just searching on Google will list hundreds of different sites that either will post a link to your ezine, or will host your articles. Here are a few:

- http://www.articlesbase.com
- http://www.amazines.com
- http://www.articlecity.com
- http://ezinearticles.com/
- http://www.buzzle.com
- http://www.1888articles.com/
- http://www.articlealley.com (requires exclusivity)
- http://www.Goarticles.com

You might consider using the paid service called www.submityourArticle.com, which takes your one article, and sprays it to many of the article directories throughout the web. There are some interesting features of this site, including the ability to trickle the articles out over time, and the ability to slightly modify each article, so that the likelihood of a lowered Google search ranking is mitigated.

Note: we are not providing any endorsement or assurance as to the quality of any of these sites. Please read the fine print carefully.

More ideas

.name domain (and other domains)

Beyond the .com, .net, .org, and other standard domains, there is a domain called ".name". As an expert or public figure, you may wish to secure this particular domain name before anyone else who shares your name does so.

The rules for purchasing the .name domain are (supposedly) different than those for others: You are supposed to register your first name as a subdomain. In my case, this means that I could only register *randall.craig.name*. Someone else could register *linda.craig.name*, and yet someone else could register *john.craig.name*.

An interesting side-note: if you are interested in becoming a Naymz premium subscriber, they will register your .name domain for you, and point the domain to your Naymz profile page. While this is a neat way to "take care of the problem", in this case, it isn't you who owns the domain, it is them. This may cause future problems for you, especially if someone with your name also signs up to Naymz, and you cancel your premium membership. It's better to own your name outright.

While not correct, there is a loophole in .name registration on some registrars' web sites, which allows you to register (and own) your entire name: eg *randallcraig.name*. You might consider doing this, if only to prevent someone else from taking it from you.

If you haven't registered your full name in a regular dot com domain (eg *randallcraig.com*) you really should do so. And if you are hoping to branch out internationally, you may also want to snap up other country domains (eg *randallcraig.ca, randallcraig.co.uk*, etc) and other special top-level domains (eg *randallcraig.net, randallcraig.org*). Ask your webmaster to take care of this for you, or try to do it yourself (it's not that hard) at either http://www.ipower.com or http://www.godaddy.com.

Ping.fm

www.ping.fm is a microblogging service that allows you to send a microblog (set your "status") to all of your social network sites – both Anchors and Outposts – all at once. Essentially you just register, then choose the social network sites that you want ping.fm to log into. To get to the entire list of social networks, after you register, click on the *Settings* link, and then click *Add Network* for those that you wish to add. Ping.fm was recently purchased by Seesmic, which makes a similar status monitoring and broadcasting product, so it isn't clear whether (or how) Ping.fm might change.

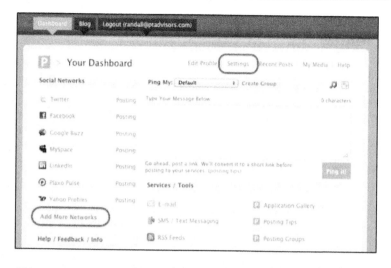

There are some other sites that do similar things (hellotxt.com is one of them), so if ping.fm doesn't seem to work for you, then try this one out. Hellotxt.com also has the interesting ability to aggregate all of your friends' microblog feeds onto one page, saving you a bit of time if you're interested in what they wrote.

At the time of writing, there was NO way to have Ping.fm, Hellotxt.com, or any other site auto-update the Google+ service. Advanced tip: If you are insistent on doing a 100% integration, there is a way to have Google+ update the Ping.fm service, which then updates all of the others. Expect this to change, but for those of you who are "experts" and wish to try, here's the outline of how to do it:

1) It is possible to update Ping.fm via email. Get your unique Ping.fm email address at www.ping.fm/email.

2) Within Google+, go to the area where you can invite your friends to your Google+ profile, and click *Add a New Person*. Write your personalized Ping.fm email address here.

3) Create a new circle, and drag this new "person" into it.

4) Whenever you update Google+, make sure that you are also including this new circle. Ping.fm will get the update, and therefore all of your other networks will as well.

Note: Test this several times, to ensure that you Google+ doesn't truncate the subject and/or number of words in your post.

Chapter Six: QR Codes

QR Codes are those postage stamp sized graphics that when read by a smart-phone reader, bring up a website (or actually, do a number of different things, depending on what is encoded.) They are a powerful bridge between real-world collateral and the Social web. Some examples:

- Put a QR code on your business card to drive people to your LinkedIn profile, personal or corporate website, or YouTube video.

- Put a QR code on your brochures and other collateral to provide more details online, or to get people to provide feedback on an issue.

- Put a QR code on a powerpoint presentation screen to have audiences go to a reference site.

- Put a QR code in the footer of each printed web page, so that people can easily go to the web page just by scanning the code.

- Don't put a QR code in an advertisement that is only available in an underground subway, airplane, etc. (It's surprising how many advertisers actually do this.)

To generate QR codes, you need a generator program. Simply Google "QR Generator" and you will find a number that are available on websites, and others that you can download. (I personally use a program on the Mac called QREncoder.app, which is fabulous.)

Type in the URL, tell it what type of QR code you want it to generate (usually it's a URL), and that's about it. Copy the resulting graphic, and paste it where it's needed.

To read the QR code, the smartphone needs a special App. Go to your smartphone's app store, and search for QR code; most are free and do a great job. Hint: Before you commit to printing hundreds of copies of a document that has a QR code in it, or before you put the QR code on the screen, test it out first.

An important note: remember that people are actually going to look at the target URL from your QR code on a mobile device. It makes sense, therefore, to send them to a cleanly designed mobile page URL – not a hard-to-read page designed for a regular laptop browser...

One of the biggest user frustrations is when their smartphones are not capable of reading the QR code itself. While they think it is their phone's fault, usually it isn't. As the producer of the QR code, it is up to you to make the code as legible as possible. This means adhering to the following guidelines:

1) Do not print shrink the size of the graphic: the smaller it is, the tougher it is for the reader to recognize. And make sure that it isn't printed over a fold, on smudgy paper, or with low contrast.

2) Use a higher error correction rate. Some encoder programs allow you to choose the error correction used during the encoding process. (You can choose between 7-30% error correction.) The higher the error correction, the more likely the reader can read the QR code, even if some of it is damaged.

3) Reduce the length of the URL: It's simple math, the fewer the characters, the less complex the actual QR code is.

Consider these examples:

http://www.randallcraig.com/six-steps-to-strategic-blogging/ (at 25% error correction)

 http://budurl.com/2hjs (a shortened URL, at the very same error correction level; note the smaller size, as there are fewer characters in the URL.)

This example is the same URL, but with 7% error correction. While this example has less in-built error correction, the physical size is smaller and the dot density is lower. This means that if it magnified and shown to an audience in a powerpoint presentation, it may actually be easier for a reader to scan from the audience, than the highly dense versions shown above.

This final example is a Micro QR code. It has even less data, and takes up even less room. We don't suggest you use these, as not all smartphone QR code readers understand Micro QR codes.

Chapter Seven: Presentations

Preparation: Whether it is a book signing, new client pitch, or a keynote in front of 1000 people, Social Media offers significant intelligence. The more prepared for the event, the stronger your impact will be.

Before events: Participate in discussion forums, conduct surveys, read Facebook or LinkedIn posts, ask target members about their issues – and about your subject area. If it is a public event, consider using your Social Media footprint to help publicize the event itself.

At events: Use a Twitter wall (see below), remind people to connect to you via Twitter, LinkedIn, or whatever your preferred Social Media venue is. Suggest Social Media resources that can help meeting attendees. If the event is public, ask if anyone wishes to *live-tweet* the event. (Live tweeting means summarizing the presentation for the Twitterverse, as you are delivering it.)

After events: Connect with people that you have developed a real-world relationship with. Tweet (valuable) information from the event to your followers. Continue the real world conversation in the social web.

Twitter Walls

These are probably the most challenging real-time use of Social Media. The idea is that a second computer and projector is set up, and that audience members can have a "back-channel" conversation using Twitter, that is displayed real-time on the second screen. The mechanism to make it work is the use of a unique #hashtag, which the second screen searches for and displays real-time.

There are several programs that can do this, but one of the best is http://www.Twitterfall.com. Remember three things when you're using this program: (1) After you enter in the #hashtag, put the program into presentation mode. (2) Change your browser to "fullscreen" mode. (3) Turn off any screen savers, energy savers, etc, so that the computer won't turn off or fall sleep during your presentation. If you don't like www.Twitterfall.com, try www.Backchannel.us.

If you are going to do a Twitter wall, here are some additional suggestions:

- Rehearse your presentation several times with a Twitter wall. It is a very challenging type of presentation, and you are better to learn without an audience, than in front of one.

- Pre-tweet a few relevant messages beforehand, so that there is at least something that is shown on the page.

- Beyond the interaction of the day, a key objective is to have people Follow you. Make sure that your address is in your presentation... and that you remind them from time to time.

- Double-check the #hashtag just before your presentation, just in case another organization has begun using it.

- Have at least one person in the crowd is specifically tasked with answering questions from people as you present. That way you don't have to side-track your presentation every time someone says something "important" via Twitter. Remember that it truly is a team presentation, and the person who is managing the backchannel needs to know how you might respond, how you define certain terms, etc.

- Arrive early to do a "pre-show", if possible, encouraging audience members to Tweet, comment, etc. If you don't do this, then someone else should. (It's not a bad idea if the session could be advertised as "...having a Twitter wall, so please bring your computers or smart phones...")

- Make sure that there is a big enough monitor in front of you as the speaker, so that you don't have to be constantly looking over your shoulder.

- Schedule specific time at key points in your presentation to acknowledge and/or address certain points on the Twitter wall.

- Well after the presentation, go online and thank everyone who Tweeted, and possibly offer them a link to one of your resources.

There are fairly strong arguments for NOT using Twitter walls, and it could be that they are inappropriate in your situation. For example:

- Attention is divided between you, the Twitter wall, your Powerpoint (if you use it), and the Smartphone. Engagement may actually suffer. This is especially true if users get sidetracked into other Twitter (or Social Media or email) activities.

- You may lose control of the audience if the backchannel discussion takes a left-turn and you cannot get the presentation back on track.

- Your lack of practice with the technology will lower your subject matter credibility

- Technology can go wrong.

Live Polling

One of the more fascinating aspects of modern presentations is "live" polling. Until recently, the only way to do this was to distribute a mini-keypad to attendees (http://www.turningtechnologies.com/ is one of the best-known providers), and then using a powerpoint plugin and a special radio receiver that plugs into your computer, the audience response would be shown within a powerpoint slide. Very slick, but also very expensive.

With smartphones and text messaging there are now interesting (and affordable) alternatives. Two of them are www.ivoted.com, and www.polleverywhere.com. Both of these companies have free trial accounts that are very quick to set-up. Both of these companies offer web, Twitter, and SMS voting, but ivoted.com only works in the USA. Polleverywhere.com works almost everywhere.

One of the caveats of using live polling in your meeting is that you will require adequate bandwidth in the room, for text-messaging, 3G/4G data, and/or WiFi: If there isn't access, then you'll get audience frustration instead of responses.

Chapter Eight: Your own Web show

Writing content is great if your target only reads. But many clients prefer to consume their information in other formats: audio and video in particular. As clients will often see you "live", not just in written form, it may make sense to consider how they can consume you in non-written formats as well.

We've already gone through the process of creating a YouTube channel. The YouTube search engine is the second most used search engine in the world; if your content is good – and is findable – you will be able to attract a number of viewers and subscribers. As a baseline solution, it may do the trick, but what if you want more? And what if the YouTube downsides are important issues for you:

- Branding is there's, not yours.
- YouTube is monetizing your content, you aren't.
- Other videos creep into "your" channel – possibly even your competitors'.
- No creation of a community of interest/no way to integrate your blog on your video site.
- No linkage outside of YouTube (eg to your expertise site)

Thankfully, there are alternatives.

1) YouTube clone services: Sites such as www.vimeo.com, www.vodpod.com, and www.blip.tv all provide free (and sometimes paid) service to host your own produced videos in your own channel. Their revenue model is the same as YouTube's, and the downside of each is also similar.

2) Web broadcasting services: these services provide a mechanism for you to have your own branded channel, on their platform. Their business model is that you provide the content, and they earn the advertising revenue. There are a number of these that exist – the two best known ones are www.ustream.com, and www.blogtalkradio.com. Ustream.com is all about capturing live streaming video for your channel. Blogtalkradio.com is more focused on providing a live radio show. Both provide limited "free" accounts, and modestly priced packages with more capacity, functionality/fewer restrictions.

3) Create a customized video delivery site: Another alternative is to develop your own "channel": a web site that is optimized to serve video, where you can develop a branded community of interest around each video episode that is created.

My firm has developed such a platform, SilverSpoke. In addition to video streaming, it also does pay-per-view video, and integrates ad management, blog aggregation, CRM, and several other features. If interested, please contact us at www.RandallCraig.com for a demo. (Sample sites running this platform include www.WisdomExchangeTV.com, www.ExtraordinaryWomenTV.com, and www.ProfessionallySpeakingTV.com.)

Producing your own video

Whichever option you choose, you still need to actually produce your own video. There are several options for this:

1) Use a webcam while sitting at your desk: Very simple, and very cheap. But very poor quality, and very difficult to integrate other guests.

2) Use a home video camera or a "flip" video camera with a tripod: Better, and it means that both you and your guest can be in the shot at the same time. Often the quality of audio suffers because of the distance of the camera to each guest.

3) Set up a mini-studio of your own: This is far better, in that you can control lighting, sound, cameras, and use a purpose-built backdrop. Downside is the cost of the hardware, mixers, lighting, and other equipment.

4) Rent studio space and production expertise: There are a number of studios that are willing to rent their studio and production expertise. Expect multiple camera angles, lav microphones, green-screen (or real) sets, professional lighting, and post-production services. Depending on what you are willing to pay (and the expertise of the studio), you can get High Definition TV quality work, or just slightly better than mini-studio-of-your-own quality.

While professionals would sniff at using consumer-grade software and equipment, we have successfully used Apple's free iMovie to do a significant amount of editing.

Chapter Nine: Advertising

While the scope of this guidebook is really online PR, it wouldn't be complete without at least a brief mention of online advertising. By online advertising, we are not referring to banner advertisements, but rather pay-per-click (PPC) contextual text advertisements: Google AdWords, Facebook Ads, and LinkedIn Ads specifically. (The beauty of PPC advertisements is that unless someone clicks them, there is absolutely no cost to you.) It is easy to find web pages that show PPC ads within a Google search, within a 3rd party web page, within a Facebook page, and on a LinkedIn page.

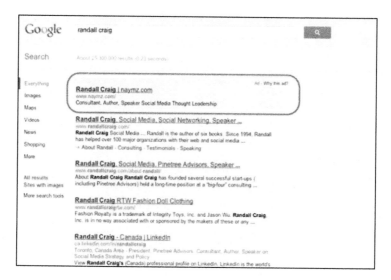

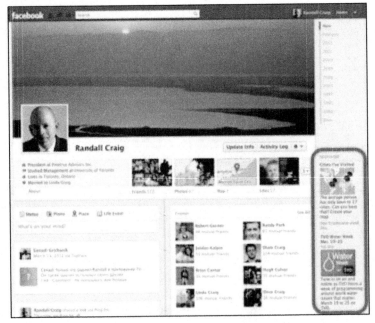

You may wish to advertise to sell your products, to solicit sign-ups to your email list, or to let prospective clients see a demo video. The overall strategy is that someone sees your advertisement with a specific call-to-action, and when they click the ad, they will be directed to a page of your choice: likely a specially-written landing page on your site that addresses the ad's call-to-action. Pay-per-click is really a win-win for you. On one hand, you only pay when they click; on the other hand, if they don't click, they can still read your message, and you gain increased awareness.

As an advertiser, you need to...

- choose keywords (which will determine where the ad appears)
- write the ad copy (about three lines)
- choose an appropriate image (for Facebook ads)
- choose a target URL (the location where the ad links to)
- bid a per-click price (which determines the relative placement of your ads, and sometimes, how often the ad will appear.)
- set a budget (which is the most that you are willing to spend)

The way these ads work is relatively simple. In Google's case, web site owners sign up to have the ads appear on their sites, in exchange for a share of the advertising revenue. Google (or Facebook or LinkedIn as the case may be) then matches the page content with your keywords. When there is a match, your ad appears. Again, as an advertiser, you are only charged when someone actually clicks on your advertisement.

The tools that are available (within Google, Facebook and LinkedIn) are impressive. You can design multiple versions of each ad copy and track their effectiveness. You can test the effectiveness of different keywords groups. You can test different geography or demographics for each ad. The combinations and permutations are endless, and can be an active, time-consuming task.

Recommendation: Pay-per-click advertising is definitely a second priority compared to all of the other activities within this guidebook. If you do it yourself, consider it more of an experiment. Much better to hire someone who has the time to do all of the optimization work. Nevertheless, if you are keen on giving it a try, here is how to get started:

Google AdWords: Assuming you have a Google account (and are signed in), click on your picture in the top-right corner, to expose the Google account drop-down menu. Choose *Account Settings* to expose your Google Accounts page. Click *Products* (3) in the left-hand navigation area. This will bring you to the page that shows all of your Google products. If you don't see AdWords, then click on the *Edit* link (4) to add it. Otherwise, click on *AdWords* to go into the system and begin placing your ads.

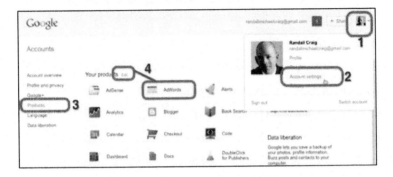

The first thing that you will probably want to do, before creating a campaign, is to decide on what keywords that you wish to use. (Check out the *Keyword Tool*.) For more instructions, please look through the detailed *Help* pages.

Facebook Ads: Log in to your Facebook account. On the bottom of every page is a link that says *Advertising*: click it. Once you are there, click on the *Create an Ad* button in the top-right corner.

The next page walks you through the process of designing, targeting, and paying for your ad. The targeting capabilities of Facebook are incredibly robust: your ad can be targeted by any combination of age, gender, keywords, relationship status, languages, education level, workplace name, and more.

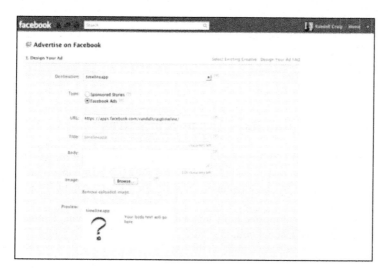

More information on how to get started can be found in the *Help* area.

LinkedIn Ads: These ads are considerably more expensive – a minimum of $2 per click – but are also more targeted to "professionals". To get to the advertising area, click on the *Advertising* link at the bottom of any page, then *Start Now* to begin.

There are three steps to go through: first, name your Campaign and creating the ad copy. LinkedIn allows you to create a number of variations that can be tested for effectiveness. Then target the advertisement to a geography, position, group, keywords, etc. Then finally set the per-click cost and a maximum budget per day.

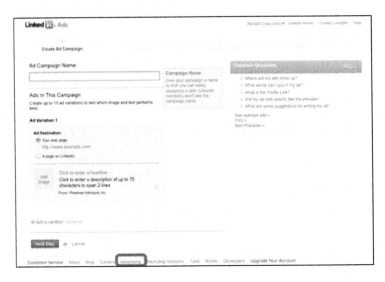

Advertising guidelines and best practices

There are dozens of books exclusively on this topic, so to do it justice requires more than just a few bullets. Nevertheless, if you are intent on using (or trying) PPC advertising on the web, consider these guidelines:

- Use a headline and body text with a clear call to action. People don't care about you; they care about the problem that you solve. Cut through the clutter on the page!

- Use an image that attracts attention, intrigues, but is still "in brand".

- Use keywords that describe either the problem or your solution. Use the Google Keyword Tool to identify related and better-performing keyword variations

- Fish where the fish are: Target your ad to the correct demographic: there is no sense advertising in an area where there are no prospective purchasers.

- Link to a landing page (eg a purpose-built page) on your web site that addresses the reason that the person clicked the advertisement.

- Split testing: Try multiple variations of headline, body text, image, keywords, and landing page to see which combination produces the highest click-through.

- Monitor your ad spend and performance on a daily basis, aiming for continuous improvement

Chapter Ten: Connecting online and traditional PR

At one end of the spectrum, developing an identity can be done using web-only social networking and identity sites; at the other end of the spectrum, there is traditional PR using a PR agency's press relationships (and releases, advisories, etc) to develop your profile. While traditional PR is beyond the scope of this guidebook, there are a number of PR-related web sites that you should be aware of, and some basic activities that make sense for you to do. Rationale:

- They will allow you to take advantage of your web profile.

- They are a great supplement to any traditional PR investment.

Here is a summary of the six services:

	Receive Journalists leads	Send out press releases	Directory	Search Engine Friendly	Annual Cost
HARO	Email list only	No	Online ($19/mo.)	No	Free/$19/49/149/month
PR Leads	Email list ony	No	No	No	$1188
ExpertClick	Direct queries only	Yes – 52 free	Print and Online	Yes	$780 (reflects $100 discount)
Profnet/ PR Newswire	Direct queries and Web list w/tracking	Yes – $$$$	Online	Yes	$1650/yr + $680 per press release
PRWeb	No	Yes - $$	No	$200+ plans	$80-$360 per release
Sources (Canada only)	No	Yes – free	Print and Online	Yes	CAD$349 +$99 photo, + $25 hotlink

HARO

HARO (which stands for *Help A Reporter Out*) is a web site/mailing list that matches journalists' queries with expert sources (like you). The web site takes your registration information, and then sends out a detailed email several times daily with journalists' queries. If a particular query matches your expertise, then you respond directly to the journalist. For a subscription of $19/month you can pre-filter the emails that are sent to you, and create an online profile.

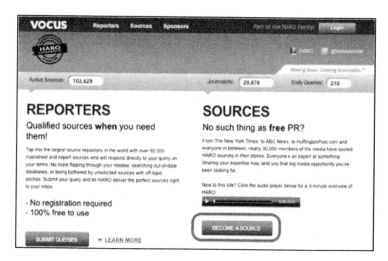

The problem with HARO is that because the cost of entry is so low (eg it can be free), any journalist who posts on the list is likely to be deluged by sources who may or may not actually be experts. Which means that the likelihood of your quote being actually used is very low. On the other hand, for $19/month, it may fit into your strategy as an Outpost site.

Recommendation: the cost is right, so sign up anyway. Consider spending a few minutes each day reviewing the queries, but only respond if you are a *perfect* match. Consider the paid service only if PR is an important part of your strategy. Sign up at http://www.helpareporter.com/

PR Leads

PRleads.com uses the same approach as HARO, except that you pay $99/month to receive filtered daily emails. By virtue of the requirement to pay, it is less likely to attract wannabe's, and more likely to attract "real" experts. Still, there isn't a way for the journalist to check your "profile" without leg-work, as this is still just an email list-based service.

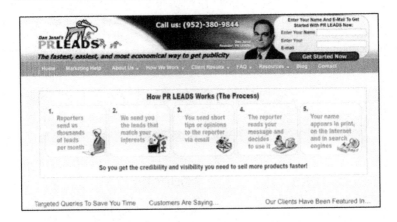

Recommendation: for about $1200/year ($950 if paid in advance), PR Leads is a lot more expensive than HARO. Consider it only after you have signed up for HARO and ExpertClick. More information is at http://www.prleads.com/

ExpertClick

About 25 years ago, ExpertClick started as a printed directory of experts and an accompanying printed directory of media. Over the last number of years, it has added an online press release distribution service and online expert directory. As an added bonus, the pages are search engine optimized, so your ExpertClick profile tends to come up very high in the Google rankings. An example ExpertClick profile:

To subscribe to ExpertClick, you need only choose which package you are interested in, and send them your check. (the cost is from $880 to $2880). The only real difference between their various packages is the amount of space that you get in the print directory... and that the more expensive packages will get you higher rankings on the site when someone does a search. All of the packages include all of the online features and no-cost press release distribution. Note that they do have a $280 package, but this does not include the directory or other benefits. We have negotiated a $100 discount (eg cost is reduced to $780) for guidebook readers. Use this special URL: https://www.expertclick.com/discount/Randall_Craig.

Recommendation: Sign up: even if you get no direct calls, the service will pay for itself through the free press release distribution capability. In addition, the benefit to being included in a third party "real" directory is that many journalists have an inherent distrust for information found exclusively on the web, and often do their due diligence with the printed directory.

Profnet

Profnet is aimed more at PR agencies, and like ExpertClick, it provides a listing of experts, ability to send PR out on "the wire", and a fair amount of other functionality.

If you are interested in reviewing this vendor, the following URL is the entrypoint: https://profnet.prnewswire.com/

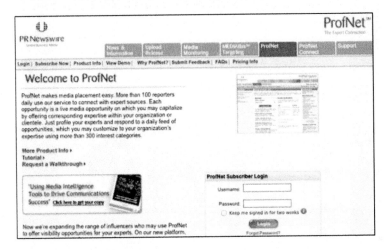

One of the benefits of Profnet and PR Newswire is that the status of each release (and query) is tracked, allowing you to more closely assess the benefit of your investment. The screen shot below shows journalist queries:

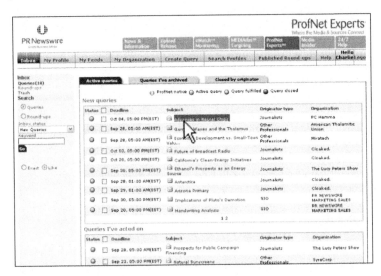

Costs are not shown on the site, and strangely, they are very difficult to obtain in a clear and concise manner from their reps. As of April 2012, the pricing for one sole person accessing the system is $1650/year to be listed on Profnet in ONE category. In addition, there is a set fee every time you send a release, which depends on which of their lists that it is sent out to. If sent to their US1 list of 5400 outlets, the cost is $680 for up to 400 words ($185 per additional 100 words); if sent out to their English Canada list, then the fee is $395 for up to 400 words. (To send to both lists, the fee is $825.)

If you are based in Canada, you can use CNW (Canada Newswire), which is the agent for the US-based PR Newswire in Canada. To send across Canada using their basic network (all major radios, televisions, and dailies), it costs $144/100 words. Adding weeklies and community newspapers changes the fee to $254/100 words. Sending to the US is $646 for the first 400 words ($142/100 words thereafter).

The pricing of these press releases seems to fluctuate based on a number of factors, including volume: use these numbers only as a rough guide.

Recommendation: Exceptionally costly, and likely not worth it for most experts. On the other hand, PR Newswire has a long-time positive reputation, and your PR agency (or your publisher's PR agency) likely has a membership. For your major events, get them to send out the release.

An interesting alternative to using PR Newswire directly is to use one of their subscriber companies to do it for you. www.Webwire.com, for example, has a distribution agreement with them that might cut their fees. Note that Webwire has several services that are not recommended – WebPost and WebRelease; if you are interested in having a true press release, look for *Targeted Media Distribution* or *Wire Service Distribution* on their site.

PRWeb

Unlike PR Newswire, www.prweb.com does not require membership, and allows you to send press releases, one-at-a-time, as you wish. Essentially, you choose your "visibility", and pay between $89 (essentially Google/Bing only) and $369 (includes regional and AP news feeds) to send one release. The release itself is also hosted on the prweb.com site, which allows for tracking statistics.

Recommendation: If you are not going to sign up for ExpertClick (which has free press release distribution services), then this is the most economical way to get your message out. If you do use the service, though, don't bother with anything less than their $199 plan.

Sources

Sources (www.sources.com) can be thought of as a Canada-specific version of ExpertClick, but with fewer integrated/automated features. While this service seemingly may not be of interest if your target market is not in Canada, Sources has done a great job with their search engine rankings, and often an expert's Sources listing page will show up on the first page of a Google search – even if the search is done on Google.com from a non-Canadian location. And this means, since there is a link from your profile page to your main web site, that your main web site will have a higher search engine ranking too.

To get the most out of a Sources listing, we recommend the following:

- Ensure that you get a hotlink from your source.com listing to your main web site.

- Take advantage of their press release distribution service.

- Sources has a number of special listings pages that you should ask to be included on. For example, they have one page for Speakers, another for Authors, etc.

- If you have a published book, ask that it be included within the "Sources Bookshelf". This will give you more exposure, and the book titles will be automatically cross-posted to your reference listing.

Recommendation: Especially if you are located in Canada, or are targeting publicity from Canadian media, we recommend that you get a Sources listing. Sign-up and registration is still done manually using a PDF form, but posting your press releases and event entries is done through the site. Fees are dependent on the size of your business, number of words in your listing, and whether you want various upgrades (photo, link to website, etc), but for most people, it should cost approximately CAD$500.

Other services

There are dozens of other services, including www.PRNewschannel.com, www.massmediadistribution.com, www.pressking.com, www.accesswire.com, and many others on Google. Here are some criteria for you to choose:

- Does it include distribution to "traditional" channels, including the AP Newswire, CBS Marketwatch, Wall Street Journal, and others. Or is it internet-site-only-based.

- Does it include a profile page for you, or is it a distribution system only?

- What are the limits regarding how often you can send? (If it is supposedly "unlimited".)

- Are there any volume discounts? (If it is pay-as-you-go.)

Social Media News Releases

The above press release distribution services offer excellent opportunities to deliver important content to journalists. However, in a Web 2.0 world, media no longer have a monopoly on which stories can be distributed. Press releases can now be created in a social media friendly format.

In traditional news releases, the text of the press release is usually (but not always) written as a news story, with an eye-catching headline and an article written in standard journalistic inverted pyramid style. The focus of the news release starts with the most important detail of the story to be conveyed in a brief and succinct sentence. From there, the "pyramid" works its way down explaining the second, third and finally the lesser important aspects of the story. This style is effective for reaching harried (and often skeptical) journalists who rarely read entire releases. It also makes it easy for journalists to lift entire passages from a release and insert them into their own articles.

In a Web 2.0 world, those seeking information and news on the web are even more stressed for time. Enter the Social Media News Release. The format of such news releases collects and shares content across various social media platforms. With different formatting than traditional releases, they also integrate your stories into the blog formats online journalists and bloggers prefer. There are many different ways to develop a social media news release, but they generally have the following elements:

- Contact information (including Skype and possibly Instant Message address)

- News release headline and subhead

- News release content (paragraphs and bullets)

- Link and RSS feed to purpose-built page, likely on a social platform (Delicious, Tumblr, or your own site)

- Multimedia examples: photo(s), MP3, graphics, video, including embed codes

- Additional information available on request: whitepapers, interviews, etc.

- Quotes from spokespersons and credible third parties

- Links to additional relevant coverage

- Sharethis/Addthis social sharing/liking links

- Links to executive's LinkedIn profiles, Twitter accounts, etc.

- Other media releases

- PR boilerplate statements

To fully benefit from the power of building awareness through traditional media relations as well as through social media news releases, we recommend crafted news releases for both formats, integrated into your organization's website.

To begin the process of formatting, creating and distributing social media news releases, you can look at www.PressItt.com and www.PRXBuilder.com. Both services can walk you through the process of building and distributing social media news releases.

Proactive PR to influential bloggers

There are a growing number of blogs and bloggers whose influence approaches, and sometimes surpasses, that of mainstream media. These blogs tend to be exceptionally narrow in their focus, speaking to a very specific audience. You probably know who they are within your area of expertise, but if not, go to Technorati and do a search. (Of course, the best case is when *you* are that influential blogger, but even when this is true, there are others who you can use to develop an even greater reputation.)

You will want to reach out to the Blogger, with the ultimate aim of them deciding to review your book, your performance, do an online interview, or otherwise credentialize yourself. There are a number of ways that you can begin to do this:

- Answer the question: what's in it for them? What will they learn? Are you giving them a scoop on a new idea or concept? They serve their readers, so unless you can quickly show alignment and relevance, you have no value to them.

- Make sure that they are on your Press Release distribution list, so that they also receive information that is aimed at traditional journalists.

- Comment on their blog postings in a thoughtful way.

- Send an email directly to the blogger suggesting an item of interest that they may wish to see or write about. (Be careful about appearing too self-serving or your proactive work can backfire. You will need to strike a balance between providing them bona fide information, and connecting the information to you or your services or book.)

- Send a copy of your most recent book for their information and background. Be aware that in some jurisdictions (such as the US), bloggers now are required to disclose any "freebies" that come their way, as well as any compensation that they receive for writing about your product.

- Recommend their blog in your blog.

- Arrange to meet at an industry event, perhaps for a meal.

- Invite them to one of your events.

- Arrange to "guest blog" for each other. Note that this typically can happen only when there is a relationship, and when your two blogs are of approximately the same reach and audience type.

- If there is someone that you know who has a strong reputation in the area – and is known to the blogger – ask that person to recommend that your book be reviewed, that you be interviewed, etc.

Whatever you do, remember that the blogger is both judge and jury: they can say whatever they want about you and your work with impunity. There are no editors, fact-checkers, or complaint departments. If they don't like your approach (or if they don't like you), they can say so, no matter who you are. Treat them respectfully.

****

Reminder note: If you are not blogging yourself, you absolutely should be. I had written the mini-course *Six Steps to Strategic Blogging* for some clients, and have made it available online: even experienced bloggers might find a few gems that are worthwhile. Register for the mini-course at http://www.randallcraig.com/six-steps-to-strategic-blogging. (There is no cost.)

Changes to your Traditional PR strategy

Here is a quick checklist of simple changes that you should incorporate into your traditional PR approach:

- At the bottom of any communications to media, make sure that you refer them to your web sites, including a special media resource page that has photos of you and your products, backgrounders, your bio, and other material. A single link to your web site home page doesn't cut it anymore. Refer back to the section on Social Media Press Releases.

- Give careful consideration to your website navigation and layout. Is everything a journalist or blogger would need readily available within one to two clicks? Make certain that contact information is easily found, and photos and news are all within the same vicinity. If you make a journalist or blogger hunt for information, you are significantly decreasing your organization's chances for coverage.

- Consider referring them to your Squidoo lenses on specific subjects, as story backgrounders.

- Consider using a "special for media" signature on all of your emails to journalists, which includes links to your LinkedIn profile, Facebook Fan Page, and media resource page.

- For media that you have a strong relationship with, ask them to connect with you either on LinkedIn or Facebook. Personally ask them if they would like to receive your newsletter. (Never sign them up without explicitly getting their specific permission!) Don't be offended if they would rather not connect with you. We have run into some journalists who have a "policy" not to connect to sources using social media.

- For radio interviews, ask the producer to add a link to one of your web sites or anchor pages from either the host's blog, or their station's blog.

- You may already know that you can "camp on" to your clients, suppliers', and other partners' press releases and traditional PR activities. Don't forget that you can do the same for their Social Media initiatives too.

- On your website, make certain that your *news* section is media and blogger friendly.

Additional resources: If you are doing PR to support a particular event, I have written a detailed white paper on Social Media for meeting planners. It describes how to use Social Media to increase attendance, improve engagement, and improve reach beyond the event itself. The paper is available through the following URL:

http://www.randallcraig.com/randall-craig-social-media-for-meeting-planners/ (There is no cost.)

Chapter Eleven: Monitoring

This topic deserves an entire book of its own – it's critical to monitor the Social Web for a number of reasons:

- **Awareness**: to find out where and how your name (or your organization's name and products) are being used.

- **Awareness of others**: to watch clients, prospects, other thought-leaders, brands, and industry issues.

- **Relationships**: to respond to Social Media posts that are relevant, both to start relationships, and expose your name – and credentialize yourself – within a community.

- **Mid-course corrections**: to assess the impact of any of your Social Media plans, and possibly make mid-course corrections.

- **Risk Mitigation**: to identify risks and then mitigate them.

- **To assess the impact of completed Social Media programs**.

There are a number of tools that can be used for this. Primary amongst the lower-cost tools are Google Alerts, Gist, Nutshell Mail, and Hootsuite. (Hootsuite.com is very similar to TweetDeck and Seesmic). We will not review the dozens of other monitoring solutions that are also available, mostly because you may not have the time or budget to properly take advantage of their capabilities. If you are interested in exploring more beyond the ones here, check out http://wiki.kenburbary.com/.

Google Alerts

When you set up a Google Alert, every time a new page is added to the Google index with your search term(s), an email is sent out to you. Go to www.Google.com/alerts to begin. Caveat: make sure that you choose how often you want Google to send out the alert: *As it Happens*, *Daily*, or *Weekly*. There is no limit on how many Alerts you can have going on at the same time. Hint: If you wish to manage your alerts after you have set them up, click the link in the Google Alerts footer.

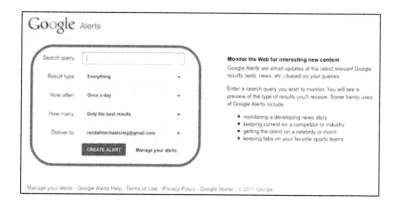

Gist

www.Gist.com bills itself as a "Social CRM" service, although it is hardly that. What it does do, however, can save you significant time. You sign up, give them your credentials to the major Social Media sites, then you wait. Each morning Gist sends you an email summary about what is happening in all of your Social Networks. Since you don't need to actually log in to each network, there can be significant time savings.

In addition, Gist has plug-ins for Gmail, Outlook, and Apps for BlackBerry, iPhone, and Android that shows the social activity of any of your contacts. (Interestingly, Gist is owned by RIM/BlackBerry, although you do not need one of their products to use the functionality.)

Finally, Gist allows you to create a public profile (including a public URL gist.com/yourname). Edit your profile to choose your profile name, connect your Social Networks, and add a few Anchor sites – it then can function as one of your Outposts.

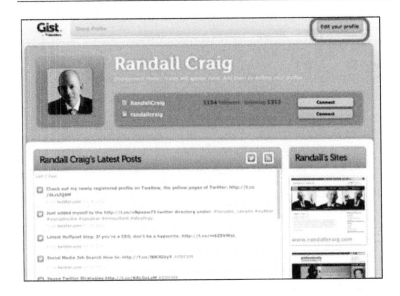

Nutshell Mail

www.NutshellMail.com is very similar to Gist.com, in that it sends out a daily update on your networks. Nutshell Mail is owned by Constant Contact, the email service provider, but seemingly is being operated as a separate, free service. To sign up, click *Create Account* in the top right corner, or the *Facebook* or *Twitter* buttons in the middle of the page.

The question of which monitoring service – Gist or Nutshell Mail – is best is a question of taste. Recommendation: sign up for both, scan both emails, and then turn off the one that you don't like as much. Or, because the information is not 100% duplicated, you can do as I do and subscribe to both. (If there is enough time, I'll scan both emails each morning, otherwise, just one.)

Hootsuite.com

Hootsuite can do two key activities: simultaneously send out a status update to Facebook, LinkedIn, Twitter, Foursquare, Ping.fm, and others. (More on Ping.fm later). Sending a status update is relatively simple: once you've given Hootsuite.com your login credentials for these other services, it's just a matter of typing your status update into the text entry area at the top of the Hootsuite screen.

The second thing that it can do is follow a conversation – they call it a stream – based on a search for certain words. Most of the functionality is free, but if you are working with an assistant, you can purchase the premium version, and delegate access.

Here's how to use it to monitor @names, #hashtags, or just plain keywords. Click *Add Stream* to add an additional column. If you already have a few streams, and just wish to change what appears within the column, click the drop-down triangle in the top right corner of the stream's column.

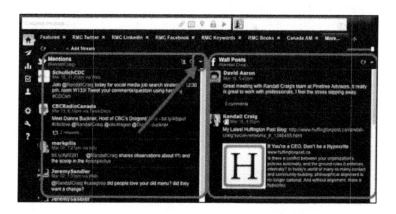

To look for, say, your name in Twitter, select *Preferences* from the drop-down menu to expose the window to Edit Streams. Click *Twitter* from the left navigation choices, then *Search*, and type in what you would like searched for.

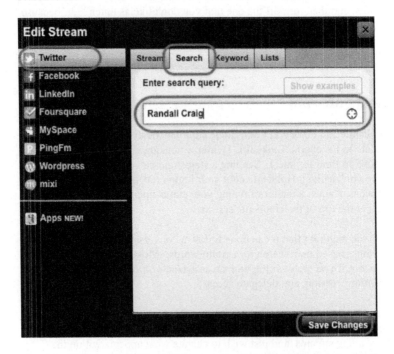

Note that if you type in Randall Craig, this will yield different results than RandallCraig (without the spaces); #randallcraig and @RandallCraig are also subtly different. Finally, click the *Save Changes* button. The main window will refresh with the changed stream. Choose *Preferences*, and add/change the nature of what is shown. When you add a stream, choosing what is shown follows a similar process.

Hint: To better organize the streams, it is more effective if you group related items into different tabs. One tab might focus on you, another might contain the names of key clients, another might contain key industry issues, etc.

Naymz

www.Naymz.com is a service that seeks to monitor your reputation over
the internet. They do this by attaching a "reputation score" (RepScore) to
you, based on the amount of information that you add to their service, the
number of references and endorsements that you develop, and your social
reach. As this service has undergone a number of substantive changes
over the last few years, it is clearly struggling, but still, it shows up in
Google search results, and is another example of an Outpost site. Their
business model will try to convince you to purchase a premium
membership, which gives you the ability to add a video to your home
page, remove advertising from your profile, and various other goodies.
One interesting perk: premium membership includes advertising on
Google keyed to your name - which may have some value..

Registering at Naymz is really a quick exercise of filling in the blanks;
don't forget, though, to link to your LinkedIn profile, your web sites, and
your blog. (When you link to your blog, your blog posts will also appear
within your Naymz profile.)

To edit the page, click on *Profile*, then click the *Edit* link just below. An
example of a completely filled out page is available at
http://www.naymz.com/randallcraig.

Klout

Separately from the above more "direct" monitoring sites, www.Klout.com deserves special mention. The goal of this site is to measure your influence over others. It does this with a secret-sauce recipe of looking at three attributes: *True Reach*, *Amplification*, and *Network Impact*. They figure this out by looking at your Facebook, LinkedIn, Twitter (and soon other) Social Networks. Sign-up is simple: from the home page authenticate yourself by clicking either the Facebook or Twitter icon.

Kred

www.Kred.com is very similar to Klout (and Naymz) in that they review your online "Influence" and "Outreach" along a number of dimensions, and give you a Kred score out of 1000 across a number of different industries. One of the main Kred determinants is your Twitter interactions over the last 1000 days. Another determinant – unique to Kred – is that you can propose Kred points for offline achievements. If you decide that Kred is part of your plan, doing this can make a significant difference in your point scores.

Functionally, Kred allows you to review/manage some of your interactions, but (in my view) it is far more efficient to do this in a purpose-built tool such as Hootsuite.

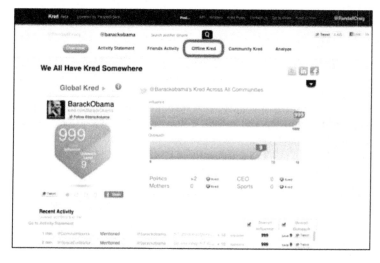

Other monitoring sites

Finally, there are several other reputation-monitoring sites that you may wish to review and/or join: there really is no downside. If you do decide to buy-in to using these (or similar) monitoring sites, we recommend that you track your performance over time, and correlate the performance with real-world activities. Only by doing this will you have an understanding of the impact (and ROI) of that particular activity.

www.PeerIndex.com: Reviews social activity and provides an index number from 1-100; depending on your influence and topics, you may be eligible for "PeerPerks". There isn't a place to add your websites, so this particular site cannot be used as an Outpost.

www.Twitalyzer.com: This service looks at all of your Tweets, and provides a dashboard of your activity, on dimensions including Impact, Engagement, Infulence, Generosity, Velocity, and about a dozen others. Beyond its own analysis, it reaches into Klout and PeerIndex to aggregate their data as well. There are some useful free reports available, but it is now largely a paid service.

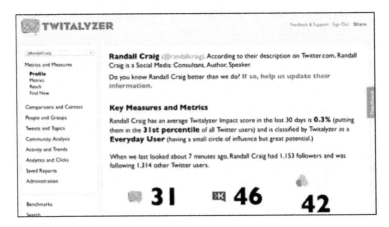

www.TweetLevel.com: Developed by the PR firm Edelman, this simple tool gives a Twitter user a rating for Influence, Popularity, Engagement, and Trust. It can also be used to analyze the performance of specific hashtags.

Chapter Twelve: Special ideas for professionals with reputation

The possibilities within Social Media are limitless. While each of the sites provides specific functionality, and serves to link the surfer both to you and to your community of interest, the great utility of Social Media happens when these tools - and they are only tools - are linked tightly to your business and marketing plan. When this happens, there can be a strong integration between real world activities, and what happens online.

Here are a small number of ideas of how Social Media can be integrated to your existing activities and initiatives:

- **Community Development and Collaborative Learning**: Create a LinkedIn group for audiences, readers, clients, or others who are seeking a greater connection to you. Post additional "bonus" materials there. For trainers, you can moderate a discussion about some pre-reading, and create a peer-based learning environment after the workshop itself.

- **Events:** Create a Facebook event to parallel the real-world one, then invite people to it. (Book launch?) Solicit input that would actually be used at the real event. Afterwards, upload event photos, tagging as many people as possible, so that the event information migrates into others' photo albums. If your prospective attendees are in LinkedIn and are connected to you by LinkedIn group membership, then you can also use the LinkedIn Events functionality for a similar purpose. (Note that LinkedIn events handle the invitation, but not posting photos, etc.) Using Polls to determine attendee preferences beforehand – or opinions after – also can improve the success of the event.

- **Awareness:** Host a contest for your readers to create a YouTube video about your book or concept, with prizes for the ones with the greatest number of votes. If you are a speaker or consultant, the videos can be about how your clients/attendees put your concepts into practice.

- **Write a *Blook*:** Consider writing your next book using your blog postings as a base. Not only does it decompress the amount of work that you'll need to do at one sitting, but your ideas will be subjected to the rigor of public scrutiny before hitting their final form. And at the same time, you'll be building up a base of potential book purchasers.

- **Promotion:** Ask all of your supporters, via email, to change their Twitter/Facebook/LinkedIn status on a particular day to recognize a cause that is important to you, or an important upcoming date: It could be a book launch, a link to a major speech, or a new report that is now available.

- **Email Communication switch:** Change from an email-only-based communication system, to one based on blog technology that allows the content to be syndicated outward, and commented on by members. Beyond general communication, this can be used to solicit comments on some of your new ideas.

- **Profiles:** For consultants who have a number of colleagues, instead of a static membership directory on the web site, add a social media component to it: let staff list connections, give recommendations, set their status, etc.

- **Business Development:** New business always comes from relationships. The transparency of your connections' connections means that you can now ask for introductions, simplify due diligence, and far more effectively prepare sales presentations.

- **Create a membership site:** These are websites in which your stakeholders pay a fixed amount each month to access your content and participate in your community.

- **Switch from email to CRM:** CRM, or a Customer Relationship Management system, is substantially different from an email lsit. An email list has the list in the center, and members "attached" to it. A CRM has the member in the middle; attached to the member is demographic and contact information, "tags", ecommerce history, list membership, and a host of other data. While Social Media is powerful at generating community, it fares poorly at driving the user to a transaction: CRM is the bridge that can make this happen. (Too often the goal is to graduate the prospect from Social Media to an email list instead.) I have written a white paper that goes into this in greater detail. To download a (free) copy, go to http://www.randallcraig.com/socialcrm-whitepaper.

- **Connect via Twitter:** Whenever you are giving a presentation, encourage your audience to follow you on Twitter, and to possibly include a Hashtag as well.

Chapter Thirteen: Ongoing management

One of the key questions you will need to answer is how active you would like to be in developing your online reputation with your audiences. Passive might mean setting it up once and doing nothing; while the sky is the limit for an Active strategy. The following suggestions are really just representative examples of what you might decide to do.

Passive Strategy:

- Annually: Update your bio on each site.

- Anchor sites: whenever a substantive change occurs in the real world, update this on your anchor sites. This may mean only 3-4 changes are made annually.

- Monthly: set aside a few hours each month to add new connections based on who you meet in the real world.

Active Strategy:

- Use LinkedIn and other tools for business development and due diligence.

- Annually: Update your bio on each site.

- Quarterly, make minor changes to your Squidoo lenses, to ensure that they remain active.

- Monthly, look through your connections' connections, in order to broaden your network to people you know in common.

- Monthly, update your Anchor sites with revised "core" content.

- Monthly, send a press release through ExpertClick; post the press release through Facebook and LinkedIn. And of course, mention it on your blog and on Twitter.

- Monthly, answer one or two questions within your LinkedIn Group (and possibly LinkedIn Answers), to develop an ongoing record of your expertise.

- Add a new video on a calendarized basis (monthly?), then link through to Facebook.

- Write a blog entry each week.

- Go through the LinkedIn Dashboard each week, and synchronize LinkedIn and Outlook. Send new invitations.

- Every 3-4 days, add a strategic new microblog "status" entry across all of your Outposts and Anchors, using either ping.fm or Hootsuite.

- Daily: Check on the status of Google, Facebook, and LinkedIn PPC advertisements, and optimize.

- Work to develop event-based campaigns, integrated with offline advertising, PR, and your real-world activities. Each of your marketing activities should cross-reinforcing.

- Participate frequently in Facebook/LinkedIn/Twitter/Google+/etc discussions.

Final words and first steps

There are many so-called gurus in the Social Media world, most who have little in the way of qualifications. Yet, there are also some great people, with great ideas, who might be completely unknown. Your success in online PR and social media is usually determined by consistently doing a number of things well, not chasing the "latest" unproven fad. The benefit of going through this book, beyond the stated intent of helping you grow your online reputation, is to help equip you with the knowledge to discern between social media common sense, and nonsense.

The amount of time that you can spend on your online profile and doing online PR can be substantial. Spend a few days going through this guidebook to set yourself up, and then calendarize a very minimal amount of time for maintenance. You can always move to an Active strategy as time goes on.

At the same time, the pace of innovation in this area is huge. Each time you log into a site to view your profile, don't be surprised to see this innovation reflected in new functionality, better layouts, and stronger interconnection between the sites. As you become more familiar with each site, you can begin to pick and choose what functionality you wish to implement. Recommendation: implement anything that provides automation and interconnection, and stay away from anything that increases your ongoing management time.